THE WAY THERE

Seeing the Journey Through

Elizabeth A. Mitchell

Scripture is from the ESV® (The Holy Bible, English Standard Version ®), copyright
©2001 by Crossway Bibles, a publishing ministry of Good News Publishers.
Used by permission. All rights reserved.

Cover Design by CathiStevenson.com

ISBN: 0692904484
ISBN 13: 9780692904480
Library of Congress Control Number: 2017909310
Way There, The, New Providence, NJ

For Pamela and Souhail Karram
who loved me first
and Joyce and Bill Mitchell
who loved me like their own

TABLE OF CONTENTS

PREFACE

As we trudge through life with burdens on our backs, mouths to feed, and hearts that ache, regular rounds of encouragement are an essential component. Sometimes big boulders loom ahead, blocking our view, causing us to feel trapped in our circumstances. Often, it is the little pebble pressed against our soles that make us stumble awkwardly as we make our way along.

When the disciples were in a tough spot on the lake with waves battering their vessel and fears drenching their spirits, Christ came to them walking on the water. He was unconcerned with the howling wind and the churning sea, the very elements that had left the fishermen fearful. Jesus stepped into their world and issued a call that still resonates with us today. "Take courage," he told them. "It is I. Do not be afraid" (Mark 6:50b).

The Lord quieted the storm and the disciples' hearts with his words. He hasn't changed. The Word of the Lord still delivers courage and soothes fears. At particularly difficult periods, when head-on collisions and crashes occur, God reminds us that our survival depends on keeping our face turned in his direction and filling our mind with his Word. He uses many portions of Scripture to reinforce this truth, but none more strategically than Psalm 105:4, "Seek the Lord and his strength; seek his presence continually!"

Seeing the journey through successfully requires gratefulness and perseverance, demands faithfulness and surrender. Sometimes the views are breathtaking and sometimes the directions are difficult to follow. Through the wilderness and on the mountain peak, the Lord remains tour guide and rest stop. He calls us to yield to detours and downpours as we pursue his plan and purposes. His hands guide us as we make our way, and he will stay with us as we journey on the way he designed for us to go. He alone provides the traveling mercies that transform our wanderings into rewarding destinations for our soul.

PART I

HIS BREATHTAKING WAYS

"For my thoughts are not your thoughts, neither are your ways my ways, declares the Lord."
Isaiah 55:8

INTERSECT

"From the rising of the sun to its setting, the
name of the Lord is to be praised."
(Psalm 113:3)

We wring our hands and fill our minds with worrisome thoughts, wrestling with God's will for our day, our future, our lifetime. What exactly would he have me do? Why doesn't he make it clear?

We read passages packed with meaty statements and struggle with how to fulfill our duties: "And now, Israel, what does the LORD your God require of you, but to fear the LORD your God, to walk in all his ways, to love him, to serve the LORD your God with all your heart and with all your soul, and to keep the commandments..." (Deuteronomy 10:12-13)

As brilliantly as the moon shimmers light through darkness, the voice of the Lord responds through his Word. "From the rising of the sun to its setting," from the moment our eyelids flutter open until they droop shut, our primary task is to praise the name of God.

We try to complicate God's simple directions. As we worship, as our minds are preoccupied with praise, we will be focused on obeying the call to love and serve him, to walk in his ways, and to revere him. As we intersect the commonplace with thanksgiving, he exchanges the ordinary and annoying and transforms the irritating and the challenging into meaning and purpose.

Rather than spending our day absorbed with the trivial, let's take the challenge from Psalm 113. Let us use the moments between sun-up and sundown to bless, consider, and rejoice in the incomparable name of the Lord.

WAVES TO WALK

"But the free gift is not like the trespass.…"
(Rom 5:15)

In the garden, Adam gambled that his way was better than the one God had designed. Along with Eve, he reached for the fruit and plucked death for mankind. We all lost big time.

God blessed these two image–bearers and commanded them to be fruitful, to multiply, to fill the earth, to subdue and have dominion over all the birds and the fish and the beasts. Rebelliously, they threw everything away.

Paul tells us Adam's choice led to our condemnation; his disobedience resulted in all of us becoming sinners. In a nutshell, "Just as sin came into the world through one man, and death through sin, and so death spread to all men because all sinned" (Romans 5:12).

Mercifully, the story didn't end in that garden. Christ entered the picture and regained far more than Adam ever lost. As Jesus walked through the hillsides and coastlines of Israel, before he even made it to the cross, he took back the dominion Adam forfeited in the Fall.

The Gospels record how the Lord had mastery over the fish that eluded Peter's nets. The experienced fishermen returned from working through the night with nothing to show. On Jesus' command to

"Put out into the deep and let down your nets for a catch," they caught so many fish "their nets were breaking"   (Luke 5:4-6).

The Lord also recaptured the dominion Adam had once had over animals. In the way we picture Adam moving fearlessly among all the creatures in the garden, for forty days Christ lived unharmed among wild animals in the wilderness (Mark 1:13). Later, when he needed transportation into Jerusalem, he rode in effortlessly on an unbroken colt (Mark 11:2).

Waves turned to walking paths beneath his feet. Storms quit their menacing force with just a few words from his lips. Diseases and evil spirits could not compete against him, deserting their occupants in quick fashion at his demand. Even the molecules in ordinary water surrendered and turned to wine at his request.

The best part was still to come. Hanging on the cross, he conquered sin; walking out of the grave, he conquered death. Paul gives a triumphant summary when he exclaims, "Christ, being raised from the dead, will never die again; death no longer has dominion over him…For sin will have no dominion over you, since you are not under law but under grace" (Romans 6:9,14).

Christ dominated. Christ overcame. Christ won. We worship!

COME AND GO

"For one's life does not consist in the
abundance of his possessions. "
(Luke 12:15b)

H is miniature hands were perfectly empty when he emerged
into our world.

Our grandson Liam drew his first breath this week, showed us his beautiful face and form, and captured our hearts the moment we saw him cocooned in the safety of his mother's arms. His delicate hands with their pink nails and softest skin were empty; he came clutching nothing in his tiny grasp.

They all come that way. Even Prince George, in his regal birthing suite in St. Mary's Hospital in London amidst a frenzy of paparazzi, brought no jewels with him. Every one enters planet Earth as Job describes: "Naked I came from my mother's womb, and naked shall I return" (Job 1:21). Every prince and pauper and precious child enters with nothing in his or her palms.

We leave that same way, too. Steve Jobs and President John Kennedy were laid to rest with bare hands, even though they had spent their days accumulating wealth, power, and significance. At the height of their careers their hands were full to the brim, but the biographical documentaries depicting their world-renowned lives tragically attest that they were consumed with laying up for themselves "treasures on earth where moth and rust destroy..." (Matthew 6:19)

Jesus calls such efforts absolute foolishness. In the parable of the rich farmer who is mesmerized by his own ability to accumulate wealth, the Lord declares this stern warning: "Fool! This night your soul is required of you, and the things you have prepared, whose will they be? So is the one who lays up treasure for himself and is not rich toward God" (Luke 12:20-21).

Earlier in the passage, Jesus cautions, "Take care and be on your guard against all covetousness, for one's life does not consist in the abundance of his possessions" (Luke 12:15). Some spend their days being "rich toward God," and others are primarily rich toward themselves. One group is mesmerized by an "abundance of possessions," whereas others are storing treasures moths will never consume and rust can never deteriorate.

Let our hands open in worship, extend in blessings, and reach to ease another's load. May we have palms that project treasures heavenward, fingers that fly to do the Master's bidding, and arms the Lord can use for his work. Until our last breath, until our empty hands lay folded on our chest, may our attention be absorbed with accumulating what he holds dear.

EFFORTLESS

*"So that you may be sons of your Father who is in heaven.
For he makes his sun rise on the evil and on the good,
and sends rain on the just and on the unjust."*
(Matthew 5:45)

O ur Creator distilled light from darkness, designed massive Mt. Everest and miniature ladybugs, and provided us a world packed with an endless panorama of perfection. Contemplating his creation presents us superb opportunities to understand our pivotal role as his children. Struck by his extravagant ways, we realize that everything from raindrops to desert sands is numberless, that incalculable reservoirs of minerals lay beneath the surfaces of earth and ocean floor. As his image-bearers, his generosity should propel us toward similar acts of generosity. Our Father's kindness should make our own arms overflow as well.

The Lord's mercy dispenses rainfall and sunshine in equal measure on the deserving and undeserving. To live with mercy as our hallmark is to mimic him. Since the Father leans forward to hear and answer prayer, to respond mercifully to a sinful people, we must also make compassion one of our primary characteristics.

Watch a snowstorm pelting sidewalks, hail hammering from heaven, or waterfalls cascading over rocky terrains. If the Lord God infuses nature with such force — if he himself is distinguished by the name Almighty — we can trust that he is more than capable of bringing order into the circumstances swirling around us.

As we consider the greatness of his character, the limitless scope of his creation, the effortless manner in which he sustains oceans deep and galaxies wide, let us walk worthy of him, striving to imitate his goodness and mercy wherever we happen to go.

MORNING MUDDLES

"If I take the wings of the morning and dwell in the
uttermost parts of the sea, even there your hand shall
lead me, and your right hand shall hold me."
(Psalm 139:9-10)

Believing a lie is easy at times. When pain is pressing down our backs, bill collectors are breaking down our doors, or a boss is breathing down our necks, we get the impression God is no longer on our side. However, the Psalms negate that thought 150 times over. Crack the Bible right down the middle, allow your eyes to dance from song to song, and you will hear the psalmists dispelling that note of discord.

King David gives form to the dim and troublesome thoughts when he writes, "If I say, 'Surely the darkness shall cover me, and the light about me be night....'" (Psalm 139:11) When fear is murkiness that conceals the face of God and appears to hinder his efforts of our behalf, midnight's colors drown all light of day.

But, look carefully now. Dark shadows and brilliant light are one and the same from God's perspective. "Even the darkness is not dark to you; the night is bright as the day, for darkness is as light with you" (Psalm 139:12). The Living God is not bound by our muddles or our midnights. When as this Psalm says, we are forced to go where morning flees away or open seas swallow us whole, verse 10 declares that "even there" his powerful hands are able to guide us safely and hold us securely.

"Even there" is where we find our God. "Even there" is where he lives and moves and breathes. No matter where life jostles us, he is "even there."

SETTING OUT

"For the LORD God is a sun and shield; the LORD
bestows favor and honor. No good thing does he
withhold from those who walk uprightly."
(Psalm 84:11)

L ike a desert wanderer who values pools of water beneath the
shade of palms, we cling to the soul-satisfying poetry displayed
throughout the Psalms. This ancient hymnbook contains 150
poems set to stringed instruments, written by more authors than any
other book in the Scriptures. It is fitting that David, the shepherd boy
anointed King of Israel, holds the record for 75 of them. Through
David's life, God reveals distinct images of the Savior.

Both claim Bethlehem as their birthplace, and both men grew
up hidden away in obscurity. Unjustly harassed and persecuted by
their enemies, both responded with acts of longsuffering and love,
triumphantly gaining victory over their adversaries in the end.
Interestingly, the titles of Good Shepherd and High King character-
ize them both.

We follow the Shepherd's leading and listen for his voice as we
drink in the meaning of the Psalms. With his staff, he protects and
directs us through the power of his Word and his abiding presence.
Unlike human shepherds who herd their sheep along, Christ lives

within us and guides our faltering steps through his indwelling Spirit. Our Good Shepherd is fully present with us for the long haul, up the steep path, through the brambles in the way.

We bow before our High King's majesty, which is on spectacular display in verses like Psalm 89:14: "Righteousness and justice are the foundation of your throne; steadfast love and faithfulness go before you." We are his beloved subjects, and we know security in his realm as he reigns in our confusing worlds.

It's a fitting tribute, then, to join the chorus of the psalmist and respond with a loud salute or a grateful whisper: "Blessed be the name of the Lord from this time forth and forever more! From the rising of the sun to its setting, the name of the Lord is to be praised!"

WINNER'S CIRCLE

"If there is any excellence, if there is anything
worthy of praise, think about these things."
(Philippians 4:8b)

Charging like a thoroughbred 'round a racetrack, our thoughts hurl from one worrisome scenario to another. With time on our hands and minds on full alert, we contemplate the dreadful, the damaging, or the difficult, assuming the worst at every turn. The medicine cabinet, glass decanter, or Internet search cannot offer sufficient remedy for such troubling maladies.

Flip the lamp switch, brace yourself against headboard or cushioned couch, and reach for the Testament propped on nightstand or credenza. On one page, in a dozen lines of print, is antidote for anxiety, relief from restlessness and choking fear.

Paul, sequestered in a prison cell and chained to Roman guards, reminds us of truth worth putting into practice: rejoice in the very place you find yourselves; rejoice some more, for it will do you good; do not allow anxious thoughts to rob you of that joy; choose prayer instead, lifting petitions large and small to God (Philippians 4:4-6).

The result of this action is worthy of a first-place-ribbon, of a garland of roses in the winner's circle. A peace that defies all understanding, that cannot be truly comprehended, will be body-guard and safety net, will put sentry at attention to protect your heart and your mind through the power of the Living Christ. This peace will transcend your situation and will cause another wondrous response in your mind and heart. Now you will be able to concentrate on what is true, honorable, and just. Whatever is pure, lovely, and commendable will be your focus and will lead you to think about the excellent and the praiseworthy, too.

Paul recommends that we continue on this circuit, that we allow the peace that comes from fixing our minds on these truths to lead the charge as we practice this ride around the paddock.

As we direct our minds to gallop in this field laden with truth, loveliness, and purity, the horse once foaming at the mouth with fear is reined in. Peace sits atop the saddle, holding the harness secure.

BEAUTIFUL WAY

"I give thanks to you, O LORD my God, with my
whole heart, and I will glorify your name forever.
For great is your steadfast love toward me..."
(Psalm 86:12-13)

She raised her arms as high as she could lift them, her face turned upward as if she saw what was invisible to others in the room. For 87 years, this mother had managed burdens of all sizes, but nothing compared to what she was now asked to bear. Willingly she had comforted her ailing daughter, standing defensively by her side to combat the cancerous onslaught. Though her prayers had not been answered the way she desired, a bitter root had not taken hold. In the sanctuary on the Sunday after the funeral, she worshiped the Lord in the beautiful way a bride gazes at her groom.

A few weeks later, when we took a meal to a young couple's home, their apartment was too quiet. When we eased the casserole onto counter top there were no baby bottles or blankets cluttering the space. Their perfectly formed son left them the very hour they first saw his precious face. No one had answers for the questions; no one had a remedy for their empty ache. We stared into their eyes and saw there a reflection of acceptance. Their peaceful demeanor and gentle words gripped us with the power of a thousand eloquent sermons. Surrender has a way of giving that startling appearance.

The psalmist echoes our deepest cry: "Give ear, O LORD, to my prayer; listen to my plea for grace. In the day of my trouble I call upon you, for you answer me" (Psalm 86:6-7). When faced with our own "day of trouble," we cannot control the outcome, even though, like David, we ask the Lord to, "incline [his] ear...preserve my life...save [his] servant...be gracious to me...gladden my soul" (Psalm 86:1-4).

In the midst of those times, we too must run toward him like a child barreling into the safety of a father's arms. Cloistered there, we are able to raise our hands in worship, even though they ache with the unknown and the ill-timed. And when we catch a brother or sister bringing glory to the Father's name rather than shaking a defiant fist in his direction, let us mimic the Lord's applause and say, "Well done. Your surrender is beauty's highest form."

POSITIONED

*"But when the chief priests and the scribes saw the wonderful
things that he did, and the children crying out in the temple,
'Hosanna to the Son of David!' they were indignant."*
(Matthew 21:15)

The little ones were singing his praises, recognizing Jesus' role
as Messiah and bursting into jubilant song right in the midst
of the temple, where the chief priests and scribes were bursting with indignant rage. The children's song must have soothed his
noble heart at a time when taxing circumstances where the order of
his day.

How peculiar to realize that those who should have known the
Scriptures best of all, who had studied the texts and memorized
the Holy Word, missed the Messiah as he stood before them. How
comforting it must have been for him to hear his praises in the very
location where his heart had been recently grieved over the greedy
merchants and money-changers desecrating the temple.

The blind and lame came to him there, and he healed them, everyone. But when they should have been applauding the miracles,
the religious ones were hissing like poisonous snakes positioned to
lunge. "Stop the children from speaking falsehoods," they demanded
of Jesus. "Do you hear what these are saying?" (Matthew 21:16)

Quoting from the shepherd boy's messianic psalm, he calmly put them in their place. Of course he heard them; they were only doing what David had prophesied about him a thousand years before: "Out of the mouth of infants and nursing babies you have prepared praise" (Psalm 8:2).

Perhaps he intentionally taunted them as he questioned, "Have you never read this part, you who are scholars of the Word, you who pretend to be the authority on the faith? Do you not recognize that I stand before you fulfilling King David's prophetic words?"

He left them then, walked away from their meanness and hatred – took himself to Bethany to escape their animosity, with the children's truthful words echoing in his heart. The young ones blessed "The Ancient of Days" with their praise and leave an example for us today. May we, too, bring pleasure to the Lord as we lift our voices to honor him in the public square, in the midst of opposition to his name.

MEANDER

"Behold, the eye of the LORD is on those who fear
him, on those who hope in his steadfast love."
(Psalm 33:18)

Some mornings, I rise before the sun, lavish my time in the reflective study of Scripture, and exercise my limbs before striding home for a nutritious breakfast. On other days, I drag my weary body out of bed, acute exhaustion already in evidence, and slouch through the day with the entire world perched between my shoulder blades.

The house occasionally appears immaculate and orderly — dust particles conquered, crumbled garments smoothed by a steaming iron, refrigerator packed with wholesome snacks. More often though, layers of grime sit conspicuously atop the furniture, bills lie stacked in cumbersome piles, and nothing nutritious beckons from within ninety meters of the kitchen door.

Periodically, my fingers fly across the keys, and the computer screen ignites with my diligent attempts at productivity. Afterward, a smile of pleasure creeps across my face at the intriguing piece before me. Far more regularly, the plastic stares back vacantly, and I meander away, distracted by my failed attempts at creating anything meaningful.

It is easy to scrutinize ourselves and discover either great lack or pride's puffed perspective. But, the Father does not grade us, is not impressed with our accomplishments or surprised by our misgivings. His love comes without conditions, without pretense or accompanying pressure.

The Master of earth and sky and everything in between is intimately aware of our short sides and long suits. He pursues us on thrilling days and in those moments when we feel unworthy. Our performance does not tip the scale in either direction; his graciousness comes with no strings attached.

He lavishes himself on our behalf, making himself accessible in our daily routine by the power of his Spirit. He is the great initiator, pursuer, and lover on those good days and those that don't seem quite so good at all.

MAKES THE WAY

"Such knowledge is too wonderful for me;
it is high, I cannot attain it."
(Psalm 139:6)

On certain extraordinary days, previously overlooked details captivate and calls me to worship: the first sip of a perfectly brewed cup of coffee; the sight of clay pots brimming with pinkish-purple impatience; birds splashing in a patio puddle like children playing poolside. In this setting, I wait expectantly, anticipating God's voice through Scripture. What sweet offering will surface today?

In the beginning of Genesis, I read of Abraham – still called Abram at this point in history – who has just blown it big by lying to Pharaoh. Cowering behind deceit and fear, he hands over his precious wife Sarai as if she were a sack of rancid grain. God quickly swoops down to the rescue, and Sarai is spared violation.

Later in the story, God tells him, "All the land that you see, I will give to you and your offspring forever" (Genesis 13:15). Abraham has done nothing to warrant God's benevolence. In fact, Abraham just made a horrific marital decision, failing miserably at keeping God's commands. Yet, in spite of Abraham's deficiencies, God extends gracious generosity toward his friend.

Abraham did not deserve God's provision; neither do we. God's response to Abraham is a reminder of his favor toward us. We do not deserve his forgiveness or his merciful kindness. We offer nothing as payment to God, and our good works and self-righteous actions do not make us worthy. He initiates, he rewards, he forgives. He makes the way for us to belong to him. Genesis lays out the gospel in those succinct words, "I will give to you."

Good morning, indeed.

TOLLS

*"But present yourselves to God as those who have
been brought from death to life, and your members
to God as instruments for righteousness."
(Romans 6:13b)*

They supposed that by conniving and deceit they could shove the carpenter into a corner, suffocate him with shavings of words, pin him with nail-pointed questions. They were the religious elite, the aristocratic Jews, and the irreligious scoffers, all plotting the demise of an irritating teacher whose lessons had uncovered their naked shame. Revenge was now their masked intent.

Jesus knew their hearts and saw through their schemes. When they confronted him on taxes, he slipped out of their noose and swung the rope back at them. The coin had Caesar's image engraved on it and therefore was to be rendered to Rome's governing body. The kingdom of earth must be supported by currency manufactured by its government (Matthew 22:15-22).

Since the Kingdom of Heaven operates with its own coinage, the King laid out a logical response. Because every human being is stamped with the image of his or her Creator, the Sovereign Lord holds claim on us. If his likeness is imprinted on us, we belong to him. What he owns must be rendered to him, for his use, for his purpose, for his eternal plan…"to God the things that are God's" (Matthew 22:21)

The scornful hypocrites did not grasp the Master's meaning. His answer stumped them, and they retreated temporarily. Still his radical message reveals transforming truth for us today.

From the Garden God declared, "Let us make man in our image, after our likeness." Carved into each one of us is the imprint of Almighty God. We are not our own, and our lives should be spent rendering back glory, honor, and praise to the One we are designed to resemble.

Go ahead. Picture yourself as Kingdom currency within the palm of God. Now, allow the Most High to spend your life how he deems best.

INSIDE OUT

"For he knows our frame; he remembers that we are dust."
(Psalm 103:14)

David's songs resonate like water heaving itself across rugged cliffs and plunging hundreds of feet to crash on river rock below; his psalms have the voice of a thousand waterfalls cascading in full force.

In the compelling language of Psalm 103, God is beyond us and yet completely on our side. Our God defies understanding and yet entirely grasps our limitations. We cannot begin to fathom his splendor and worth; he is revealing himself, unveiling himself, marking us with a love without the slightest limitations. He is Father, bending low, sweeping us close, showing compassion to our finite form. Our days disintegrate like faded weeds, our brief impact barely more than wind scattering fallen leaves. We disappear and hardly leave a trace behind; he remains everlasting, unending, perfect, and permanent.

We find ourselves in a pit; he is redeemer and rescuer. Disease clings to us, and his hands heal and restore. We are stained by iniquity from birth, but he provides forgiveness and righteousness without ever dangling it before us as reminder of our wretched past. He is altogether in the business of removing our transgressions in that spectacular, incalculable fashion, measured as far as east is from west.

Because he is "Merciful and gracious, slow to anger and abounding in steadfast love...he does not deal with us according to our sins, nor repay us according to our iniquities." In contrast, his love for us is as measureless as the distance between heaven and earth; the cost of this healing and redemption he placed squarely on the sacred shoulders of his Son.

Phrase upon phrase, the psalm escalates and celebrates the elaborate, complex nature of our God. Here is a call to worship him intimately and extravagantly for who he is and particularly for how clearly he understands us. Knowing our frame, remembering that we are dust, he crowns us with mercy, satisfies us with goodness, and renews us to soar as if we had the power evident in eagle's wings.

From the inside out and from the deepest part within, may our lives bring blessing to our good and gracious God. Made of dust and yet made to honor our Maker and our King.

STRIVING

"The heavens declare the glory of God, and
the sky above proclaims his handiwork."
(Psalm 19:1)

Every human being breathes beneath the awning of heaven
and is confronted relentlessly with the speech of stars and
planets, clouds and wind, searing sunshine and luminescent
moonbeams.

Rainfall, thunderclaps, and snowstorms declare God as glorious,
mighty, brilliant, ordered, and complex. Ultimately, he defies understanding, his startling beauty and intricate purposes mirrored in the
splendor of his handiwork.

We need only cast our eyes upward into the heavens, contemplate
the endless blackness surrounding the twinkling planets, or gaze
across the measureless mass of ocean lapping rhythmically on the
threshold of coastlines worldwide, to agree with the psalmist's declaration: "Day to day pours out speech, and night to night reveals
knowledge. There is no speech, nor are there words, whose voice is
not heard" (Psalm 19:2-3).

He calls us to cease our daily striving and surrender some time to
contemplate the intricacies of nature; the complexity of the cosmos
allows us to hear the undeniable message that God exists and God is

good. To meditate at midnight or rouse from slumber to stare into the mist-shrouded beauty of dawn is to be awakened to the sound of God's voice of reason. His creation opens a spectacular window through which we can view his character and attributes; the view should prompt worship and delight.

God of all Creation, we lift our voice to join the chorus of starlight in night sky to acknowledge your goodness and greatness with our words, inadequate and insufficient though they may be.

BRAGGING RIGHTS

*"I will extol you, my God and King, and
bless your name forever and ever."
(Psalm 145:1)*

Forever begins today in the place where regular routines pile up like day-old dishes. When I pause to wonder what God's will is or where he wants me occupied, I have only to settle my sight on one of David's songs to hear God's strong voice serenading the plan into my ear.

I hardly begin reading Psalm 145 before he directs me to what is clearly sweet and good. "Every day I will bless you and praise your name forever and ever" (Psalm 145:2). Surprisingly, I am to bless the Creator, and not the other way around. Scripture invites me to bring him the blessing of adoration on a daily basis, when it rolls out easily and when that might be the last thing on my mind.

Why should I take this seriously? The third verse gives an answer: "Great is the LORD, and greatly to be praised, and his greatness is unsearchable." The limitless grandeur of our God cannot be measured and it simply demands that we take notice and linger long in response to his perfect character. That might take a while. It's no wonder "every day" is part of the equation.

Part of my assignment is to pass on this awareness to those growing up within the safety of my arms. "One generation shall commend your works to another, and shall declare your mighty acts" (Psalm 145:4). One of my missions is faithfully to recommend to those in my care the pursuit of the Living God. I get the chance to brag about Almighty God to the children listening in.

Where should my thoughts dwell when future fears and present irritations commandeer my mind? David answers, "On the glorious splendor of your majesty, and on your wondrous works, I will meditate" (Psalm 145:5). If my thinking runs on the course of his splendid, glorious ways, my life cannot help but soar beyond the tedious and the tyrannical.

When I are tempted to believe the Lord is far removed from my everyday concerns, that my struggles are inconsequential on his scale, the shepherd king reminds me, "The Lord is gracious and merciful, slow to anger and abounding in steadfast love. The Lord is good to all, and his mercy is over all that he has made" (Psalm 145:8-9).

Gracious and merciful, patient, loving and good. That's just a sliver of the character of the God who calls me his. "All your works shall give thanks to you, O LORD, and all your saints shall bless you!" (Psalm 145:10).

Me, too, Lord. I join the chorus of the saints who bring you praise today — practice, I imagine, for what I will be doing forevermore.

SHOULDER WIDTH

*"I am poured out like water, and all my bones are out of
joint; my heart is like wax; it is melted within my breast."*
(Psalm 22:14)

Sometimes major characters consume the stage, their every
word pivotal to the unfolding narrative. However, to remind
us that ordinary folk are also essential to the story line, God
allows a minor player to teach us grand lessons worth applying to the
common rhythm of our routine lives.

In the final chapter of 2 Samuel, King David blundered big. God
unleashed severe judgment on David for acting in disobedience and
demanding a census of all the fighting men in his kingdom. Seventy
thousand of the warriors David had just foolishly cataloged were
struck down. God insisted David build an altar at the exact location
where the Lord had mercifully intervened.

Surprisingly, a brilliant picture of worship surfaced, but from a
man whose name we hardly recognize. His name was Araunah and
he owned the property designated by God for the altar. In his right
response of running toward King David and falling at his feet, we see
how humility acts when confronted with royalty. This eager servant
asked David what he could do for him and then willingly offered everything necessary. "Here are the oxen for the burnt offering and the

threshing sledges and the yokes of the oxen for the wood. All this, O king, Araunah gives to the king" (2 Samuel 24:22-23).

The man kept nothing back. Though David refused Araunah's gracious offer, saying, "I will not offer burnt offerings to the LORD my God that cost me nothing," the man's posture and sacrificial response gave us a perfect picture of true worship.

Background people shoulder important roles: the little boy on the side of the hill extended his sardines and barley bread to the Lord; compassionate Simon of Cyrene shouldered the load for Christ as he staggered to the cross; and Araunah threw himself at the feet of High King David without a thought to the cost involved.

May we too strive to imitate these lesser-known characters who reveal what the King of Heaven and Earth rightfully deserves.

RARE VIEW

*"We will not hide them from their children, but tell to
the coming generation the glorious deeds of the LORD,
and his might, and the wonders that he has done."
(Psalm 78:4)*

We call him Wonderful, and it suits him perfectly. God never ceases to perform wonders on man's behalf. Let us open our eyes to the wonderful productions displayed in every crack and crevice of our world; open the Word, and his wonders leap out like a sure-footed gazelle prancing across the plains.

As the psalmist retells the Israelites' story of redemption, God is at center stage, orchestrating wonders on every side for his people. The Lord is sea-divider and water-tamer to facilitate the Israelites escape from the Egyptians. He is cloud- coverer and night-lighter to ward off sunstroke and ferocious desert wildlife. To satisfy their thirst, he is rock-splitter and water-gusher in order for them to, "drink abundantly as from the deep" (Psalm 78:13-16).

Rather than celebrate their good fortune in a rousing worship anthem, the Israelites respond like bratty toddlers in a full-scale tantrum. They become desert rebels and God-testers. Before their abundant and benevolent rescuer, they morph into food-cravers, promise-doubters, and God-scoffers. In a word, they become unbelievers wrapped up in their own petty needs.

Yet, Jehovah remains unchanging. We learn that he is sky-commander, heaven-opener, and manna-provider. With absolute authority, he is abundant benefactor, wind-controller, meat-flinger, and craving-fulfiller.

They sinned; God judged. They repented; God forgave. They tested, provoked, and grieved the Lord, and in response, "He, being compassionate, atoned for their iniquity and did not destroy them; he restrained his anger often and did not stir up all his wrath" (Psalm 78:38).

In their rebellious hearts we see a reflection of ours, their unbelief a mirror image of our own. Rather than pouring out his well-deserved wrath against us, he poured all of it onto his Beloved Son. In like fashion, he, being compassionate, atoned for my iniquity.

Wonderful is hardly sufficient to describe such wonder-working love.

SPRINTING

"For you were slain, and by your blood your
ransomed people for God from every tribe and
language and people and nation...."
(Revelation 5:9b)

In the midst of the Olympic fervor, we find ourselves in the bottom part of Africa, in the dry and brittle month of August, where every green blade of grass has waved a flag of surrender. On the television screen, the patriotic athletes engage in robust competition in brilliantly lit London town; in rural Kabwe, the various ministries from this gathering of African nations surround each other with enormous arms of support, with cheers that rival stadium-level uproars.

In tightly crammed quarters, the crowds overflow into vinyl tents and give enraptured attention to travel-weary speakers who have maneuvered their way to the Zambian conference. South Africans pray blessings on the workers from Zimbabwe, the enthusiastic Mozambique leader is affirmed with applause, and the Malawi contingency explodes with exuberance for the task at hand.

When the petite lady from Madagascar holds the microphone, her quiet demeanor cannot veil her lion's heart, her zeal for her nation, her uncontainable longing for the unreached peoples that are imprisoned inside pagan walls. In this land where travel is taxing, where workers are few, she charges ahead like a valiant warrior forging deep into enemy territory, giving little thought to the rigorous sacrifice involved.

No one is threading medals around their necks at the moment, in the middle of the race, as they lunge around the track, sprinting for all they're worth for the cause of the Gospel. No television crew records their heroic exploits on behalf of the Savior they hold dear; at breakfast tables, we will not gaze at their faces plastered on cereal boxes.

For this moment in time, their shoes are simply threadbare from the agonizing wear and tear in the field the Lord of the harvest has called them to till. They know the cost of selfless struggle, of bravery borne on the backside of the continent, of a relentless pursuit of things most noble, worthwhile, and fruitful.

Their faces shine with the unexplainable pleasure of pursuing the prize valued in heaven's arena: the souls of men and women from every tongue, tribe, and nation who will one day worship in the throne room of the King.

PART II

DIRECTIONS FOR THE WAY AHEAD

"Make me to know your ways, O LORD,
teach me your paths."
Psalm 25:4

PERFECT PLAN

*"He sent from on high, he took me; he
drew me out of many waters."*
(Psalm 18:16)

In an attempt to explain life, we toss inaccurate phrases randomly into our conversation. "God never gives us more than we can bear," is one such repetitive fallacy. For many of us, life dumps situations that are completely unbearable and clearly beyond our capacity to cope.

King David would concur. Throughout the Psalms, he introduces us to one overwhelming scenario after another; enemies, false friends, and hardships threaten to extinguish the breath within his lungs. We sympathize with his lament: "The cords of death encompassed me; the torrents of destruction assailed me; the cords of Sheol entangled me" (Psalm 18:4). Surrounded, assaulted, entangled — David describes exactly how we feel.

Through David's poetic songs we learn that God allows us to experience incredible difficulties to direct us to rely on his mercy. Following the psalmist's example, we cry to the Lord for help, cognizant he is our only source of rescue.

His response is not marred by pity or a sense of duty. Rather, we celebrate in realizing he rescues us because he delights in us. The

God of heaven and earth exudes great joy in reaching down and making a way for us to endure, to persevere, and to survive the struggle.

"This God – his way is perfect; the word of the Lord proves true; he is a shield for all those who take refuge in him" (Psalm 18:30). Father, in the middle of the mess we can celebrate your perfect ways that defy understanding. We cannot figure you out and we cannot make sense of our circumstances. But you have it covered, every incomprehensible piece of the puzzle. As your children, we will keep our gaze on you.

TRANSFER

"Heal me, O LORD, and I shall be healed; save me,
and I shall be saved, for you are my praise."
(Jeremiah 17:14)

W hen the scars are visible, when the diagnosis is made public, we are more prone to expose our ache to others and to plead relentlessly for healing from the God of the Universe. The hidden hurts and deep wounds we dare not divulge, we unwisely believe lie beyond the Father's ability to restore. Rather than revealing the extent of our agony to him, we cower behind it, assuming the enormity of the pain disqualifies us from healing. Foolishly, we think our trial beyond the scope of the "man of sorrows, and acquainted with grief" (Isaiah 53:3).

Sometimes, we justify our malaise with a full-blown excuse for self-pity. *This horrible situation may be the lot of others, but should never have landed in my lap. My doorway should never open on to this wretched scenario, no matter what.*

Self-pity is primarily pride wearing a droopy disguise. This sense of injustice is a cry from one who shakes his fist at God and declares, "You are not the boss of me. You cannot expect me to accept this from your hand. Give it to another. I determine what is right and fair."

Wouldn't it make more sense to transfer our losses onto the one who has "borne our grief and carried our sorrows...was wounded for our transgressions...was crushed for our iniquities?" (Isaiah 53:4-5) Aren't the shoulders that carried the cross up Calvary's hill perfectly suited to manage our load as well?

The size of the problem is irrelevant to him. Hand it over – all of it. Our Savior and Healer will take it from there.

WRONG TURN

*"Is this not the reason you are wrong, because you
know neither the Scriptures nor the power of God?"*
(Mark 12:24)

The Saducees often attempted to stump Jesus. They never
could. No matter the farcical tale they threw at him, he easily read through their intent and revealed their true motives.
In Mark 12, they weaved an imaginary story of a woman who mar-
ried seven brothers consecutively, when one by one the brothers die.
"In the resurrection, whose wife will she be?" they queried Jesus.

With one succinct response, the Great Physician diagnosed their
precise spiritual malady and surgically sliced through their nonsense.
They were dead wrong on two pivotal accounts: they were completely
unfamiliar with the Scriptures and with God himself.

Most of our derailing falls into these two categories as well.
Usually, when we are off base or clueless in our choices, the root problem stems from not knowing and applying God's Word and not experiencing God's power. Like the Saducees, we like to throw him
incredulous questions. Why is this portion of my life disjointed? Why
are you making me wait? How can I manage this rotten situation?

Jesus bends his mouth close to our ears and whispers through the
psalmist, "Your word is a lamp to my feet and a light to my path...The

unfolding of your words gives light; it imparts understanding to the simple" (Psalm 119:105,130).

Father, into my cloudy thoughts beam the brightness of your Word. Spread your light before my feet so I discern exactly where you want me to go.

GUIDED TOUR

"I will instruct you and teach you in the way you
should go; I will counsel you with my eye upon you."
(Psalm 32:8)

D ressed in helmets and life vests, our family grabbed our pad-
dles and submerged our raft in the Ocoee River of Cherokee
National Forest in Tennessee. We inhaled deeply as the
white water swirled around our inflated boat and splashed us from
head to toe as we maneuvered down the swirling, rocky riverbed.

What could have been a traumatizing ride became an exhilarat-
ing adventure, packed with delightful, scenic beauty. Where we could
have been injured by the dangerous boulders or swept overboard by
the raging rapids, we experienced instead a thrilling family expedi-
tion. Our confident, well-equipped, and able-bodied guide made all
the difference.

This mountain man, with 22 years of experience directing rook-
ies like us, knew every boulder by name and could navigate safely
through the most dangerous waters without a single mishap. His
strong arms kept us inside the boat, and his intricate knowledge of
the river's layout gave us confidence to trust his directions in the
midst of harrowing spins and turns.

To stay on the riverbank and watch the action-packed scenario would have been safer, easier, and much drier. But, we would have missed out on this life-sized, fun-filled exploit. By trusting our guide's every directive, by listening to his expertise, and by following his precise words, we made it through a treacherous course uninjured and supremely elated.

Our river guide taught us a thing or two about rafting and safety, but more significantly, he reminded us about the inestimable value of having Jesus as our faithful Guide. Our Shepherd knows the way, is familiar with every curve and rapidly flowing course, and has the power and wisdom to guide us safely through. As children of the Living God, we get to follow his lead, listen for his voice, and be protected by his capable arms.

Life's unpredictable currents and dangerous curves are still controlled by the voice and the hand of our Sovereign Guide.

IGNORING THE SIGNS

*"But from there you will seek the LORD your God
and you will find him, if you search after him
with all your heart and with all your soul."*
(Deuteronomy 4:29)

We shy away from the ominous Old Testament books of the Law, preferring the gentler tone of the Epistles and the story-like quality of the Gospels. We ignore the ancient pages, believing them to be riddled with the wrathful vengeance of an angry God. Unfortunately, in so doing we grievously dismiss the God of Abraham, Isaac, and Jacob and forego the opportunity to acquaint ourselves with the flawless character of our Heavenly Father.

Some of the most endearing phrases leap out of books like Deuteronomy where the God of the Universe visibly displays relentless love for the Children of Israel. "He encircled him, he cared for him, he kept him as the apple of his eye. Like an eagle that stirs up its nest, that flutters over its young, spreading out its wings, catching them, bearing them on its pinions, the LORD alone guided him...." (Deuteronomy 32:10-12). Beyond the powerful poetic imagery, this passage offers an intimate view of Almighty God.

By the mouth of Moses, the Lord God warned his children not to stray, not to succumb to idolatry, not to wander into disobedience.

Like a compassionate father, God relayed the tragic consequences of turning away from his commandments. Yet, in the very same breath he reminded them he would be willing to extend them forgiveness. "For the LORD your God is a merciful God. He will not leave you or destroy you or forget the covenant with your fathers that he swore to them" (Deuteronomy 4:31).

Contemplate the richness of these Scriptures, picture the tenderness of the Father, reflect on his immeasurable capacity to forgive, and recognize afresh the limitless love of the God we serve. It's amazing that we get to belong to him, too.

The passion, forgiveness, and grace he extended to the wandering Israelites, he demonstrates to us as well. His Word is saturated with promises fulfilled, covenants kept, and relationships rescued through his initiative. That's reason enough to make our way through the unfamiliar pages of the love letters he left for us to live by.

STEP FORWARD

*"Therefore, as you received Christ Jesus the LORD, so walk
in him, rooted and built up in him and established in the
faith, just as you were taught, abounding in thanksgiving."
(Colossians 2:6)*

We like to believe we can accelerate ahead, feet barely
skimming the floor, making progress like a champion
racehorse bound and determined to cross the finish line
at a record pace. But, life is far more often a plodding, one sole up
and one sole down, movement characterized by faltering steps and
daily decisions to endure and proceed.

In the particular way we surrendered to Christ as Lord and
looked to him for salvation and life eternal, we are called to make our
way through life. With a lifestyle patterned after his, keeping in step
with his example, staying close by his side as we develop spiritually, we
measure our progress by his standards. We are summoned simply to
keep walking with the Savior.

Unlike tumbleweed that is blown about, the Lord reminds us to
be firmly rooted in his rich soil and to draw spiritual nourishment
there. Since Living Water and Bread of Life are two of his names, and
the Scriptures are referred to as "the sincere milk of the Word," it is
to our distinct advantage to hunker down in his presence, to linger

long with his sacred writings in order to be completely saturated and satisfied with his Truth.

The purpose he has for us also involves building, layer upon layer, a framework upon his foundation. Nowhere is the concept more clearly stated than in 2 Peter 1:5: "For this very reason, make every effort to supplement your faith with virtue, and virtue with knowledge, and knowledge with self-control, and self-control with steadfastness, and steadfastness with godliness, and godliness with brotherly affection, and brotherly affection with love."

The next verse sums up how to reach the finish line with flying colors: "For if these qualities are yours and are increasing, they keep you from being ineffective or unfruitful in the knowledge of our Lord Jesus Christ."

Walking, rooting, building – step forward and watch him work.

THE OTHER SIDE

"Blessed be the God and Father of our Lord Jesus Christ,
the Father of mercies and God of all comfort."
(2 Corinthians 1:3)

After we have pushed through the entanglements of a dense forest, arms scratched from the impact of straggling branches, head bruised from colliding with low-lying limbs, muscles whining from the strain of the fight, we emerge differently than when we first entered this wooded enclave. Armed with experience and with a clearer understanding of what the trek entailed, we approach other weary travelers with a welcome gift they, too, might choose to slip into another's palm someday.

At times, our loving Father bids us to enter the treacherous places, and we recoil at their ghastly intrusion in our lives. What good could ever come from such a darkened landscape? Why must there be stretches of complicated pathways, with the unknown looming at every turn? At first, we attempt to flee this wretched zone, to hurtle through and reach the other side unscathed. Instead, the submerged roots snarl our feet, the unexpected winds blow fiercely, and we fall face-down, buried in decaying leaves and blackened soil.

When we believe that all is lost, that circumstances have driven us miles off course, the Lord of all reaches through the messy foliage and makes us aware of his prevailing presence. The forest leaves do not evaporate; the cumbersome trunks still stand, menacing and large. But, guided by his capable hands and strengthened by his powerful arms, we make our way through, bandaged and bruised, to the other side.

All the way there, with each step around each muddled curve, he has bent his head to ours and spoken strength into our fragile places. He has cradled us within the secure crook of his arm, reminding us in written Word and living Spirit that his name is Comforter and Friend, a Brother born for adversity.

When meadows and rolling hills come into view, when the forest stands afar off and the scent of danger has slowly withdrawn, we are left with a bundle to manage. When he walked beside us and offered balm for our wounds, he eased into our hands a vial that he calls us to dispense generously. Our hands are now shaped to the task; our lips yield what he filled from the deep reservoirs of pain.

"Who comforts us in all our affliction, so that we may be able to comfort those who are in any affliction, with the comfort with which we ourselves are comforted by God" (2 Corinthians 1:4).

TURN TOWARD

"Give ear to my prayer, O God, and hide
not yourself from my plea for mercy!"
(Psalm 55:1)

Whining rarely benefits the one enduring the gripe or the complainer intent on unloading her prevailing mediocre circumstances. Who really even cares when the boss is unjust, the landlord greedy, or the neighbor's piercing accusation slices like a wretched razor blade?

God does. David adamantly insists that we recognize this trait about the Almighty in almost every stanza of his laments recorded in the Psalms. All by itself, Psalm 55 is a sacred script to review each time the weight presses against your chest: "Attend to me and answer me; I am restless in my complaint...my heart is in anguish within me...I would hurry to find a shelter from the raging wind and tempest."

Our Father in Heaven longs for us to turn toward him with the expectation of a child barreling in the direction of his parent's protective embrace. The parent who whispers encouragement into the youngster's ear or the teenager's troubled heart or the young couple's cluttered world beautifully imitates the perfect parenting of God himself.

"But I call to God, and the LORD will save me. Evening, morning and at noon I utter my complaint and moan, and he hears my voice. He redeems my soul in safety from the battle that I wage" (Psalm 55:16-18). Time and again, we are directed to bring our complaints to him, knowing he not only listens to our aching words but is also fully capable of pulling us through the skirmish. My God not only hears me out, but also helps me out as well; he can do no less.

Near the end of the psalm, we see a perfect remedy: "Cast your burden on the LORD, and he will sustain you…." We are responsible to cast it all – the bulky boulders too cumbersome to cradle and the slight pebbles, painful and unnerving. He is the one in charge of all the necessary sustaining.

When faced with insurmountable odds or merely irritating infractions, cold sweat and sweaty palms in abundance, point your furrowed brow and throbbing temples squarely in the direction of the Counselor who has ears to hear, arms to heal, and a heart of extraordinary love and compassion.

CHOOSING SIDES

"Wisdom cries aloud in the street, in the markets
she raises her voice... 'How long, O simple ones, will
you love being simple? How long will scoffers delight
in their scoffing and fools hate knowledge?'"
(Proverbs 1:20,22)

Fools revel in making idiotic choices. One of their distinguishing traits is a propensity for listening to the noisy clamor of other fools, even as close-at-hand wisdom struggles to make her voice heard. With lopsided dunce caps pulled down over their foolish ears, the note of reason becomes a distant mumble.

The book of Proverbs specializes in nonsense awareness and eradication. From its opening verses, King Solomon illustrates the main difference between one with wisdom and a foolish counterpart: "Let the wise hear and increase in learning, and the one who understands obtain guidance... but fools despise wisdom and instruction" (Proverbs 1:5,7). By their choice, fools mock at the precipice of their treacherous downfall.

Elijah was surrounded by such a pack of fools in I Kings 18. Faced with 450 prophets of Baal at Mount Carmel and wanting the Israelites to recognize the disastrous consequences of bowing before false gods, he challenged the prophets to a competition of sorts. Two altars and two bulls, with their diametrically opposed objects of worship, would collide in a showdown to determine whether Baal or Jehovah reigned supreme.

From early morning till high noon, the prophets begged Baal to answer their pleas. "But there was no voice, and no one answered. And they limped around the altar they had made." Then they cried loudly, sliced themselves with weapons of war, and raved repeatedly for some response. Again, "There was no voice. No one answered; no one paid attention."

Elijah drenched the altar to Almighty God with twelve jars of water and pleaded, "Answer me, O LORD, answer me, that this people may know that you, O LORD, are God." Only one offering was consumed with fire; only the God whose voice had spoken the universe into existence responded to prove himself before his people. The bull, the wood, the stones, the dust, and every drop of water disappeared when Jehovah showed up to defend his name.

Fools still create clamor and confusion to squelch wisdom's speech. They still limp around self-made altars while the gods of their own invention give silent testimony to their worthless state.

In dramatic contrast, in Jesus Christ "are hidden all the treasures of wisdom and knowledge" (Colossians 2:3). Solomon, Elijah, and Paul point to this grand truth: "And because of him you are in Christ Jesus, who became for us wisdom from God, righteousness and sanctification and redemption" (I Corinthians 1:30).

Hide us within the treasures of your wisdom, dearest Jesus. Drench us with the outpouring of yourself just like Elijah asked so the people in our life may also realize that "You, O LORD, are God."

STEADY RAILS

"But the serpent said to the woman,
'You will not surely die.'"
(Genesis 3:4)

Bare-armed, she reached for the fruit, yanked it free, and tumbled down an unchangeable course, wrenching all of us along with her in that sudden, devastating fall. Eve, deceived by the Deceiver in his enticing regalia, lured her husband too. Together they took a turn forever-far away from the one the Creator had designed.

Up to that point in the garden, Adam and Eve had trusted that God knew what was best. When Satan bent their ear his way, they decided that God was no longer sufficient to make the right decisions. They took matters into their own hands, believing the lie that somehow God had been keeping the best from them. They believed the serpent's savvy speech rather than the Creator who spoke intimately with them "walking in the garden in the cool of the day" (Genesis 3:8).

Somehow their example trickles down and clings to me. I mimic this pair each time I reach outside the realm of his design, the repercussion of their rebellious choice evident in my longing to decide for myself what is worthwhile. The Lord left me his sacred Words as lamppost and siren, as blazing midnight stars to illuminate the dark canopies and dangerous terrains. Yet I squeeze my eyelids tight, trusting my own blindness rather than the radiance he provides.

The Lord, mindful of my propensity for foolish ways, gives me guidelines and steady rails to lean on. "Abhor what is evil; hold fast to what is good…rejoice in hope, be patient in tribulation, be constant in prayer." He left us two Testaments packed with satisfying fruit to draw sustenance from, and to nourish others along.

In our hands are hidden living Words from for the cool part of the day, the high-beamed noontime, and the darkened cover of nightfall.

PROMPT

"I am the good shepherd. The good shepherd
lays down his life for the sheep."
(John 10:11)

S hepherds sacrifice for their sheep. Good shepherds sacrifice everything. Jesus is the greatest Good Shepherd of all. Every sheep in his pasture knows that firsthand, and he longs for the lost ones to know it, too.

Psalm 23 is the most famous account of God's flawless shepherding skills, but it is hardly the only one. For instance, when we graze across Psalm 51, we gulp enormous portions of how God purifies us, washes our wounds, and combs pests out of our tangled wool. "Have mercy on me, O God, according to your steadfast love; according to your abundant mercy, blot out my transgressions. Wash me thoroughly from my iniquity, and cleanse me from my sin" (Psalm 51:1-2). In mercy, he bends his knee and comes to our rescue, applying his healing ointments with gentle shepherd hands, removing the damages we have inflicted on ourselves.

When enemies approach, in forms not unlike ravenous wolves or prowling lions, we beg rescue. The psalmist gives words to our relief: "He sent from on high, he took me; he drew me out of many waters.

He rescued me from my strong enemy and from those who hated me, for they were too mighty for me" (Psalm 18:16).

At once both gentle in his care and fierce in protection of his flock, the shepherd only does us good, on every side of every field and every pasture we wander through. We respond, "But we your people, the sheep of your pasture, will give thanks to you forever" (Psalm 79:13).

Some things a lost sheep might need to recall to prompt him to scamper home.

RIVER WASH

*"I desire then that in every place the men
should pray, lifting holy hands...."*
(I Timothy 2:8)

Jacqueline's hands are dirty, but she doesn't care. She is four, with river sand plastered to playful fingers; she's dug a hole, carved a space in mushy soil. It is Sunday, without stiff shoes or hardwood pews.

The stream catches our eye as we explore the tiny town. The four families vacationing together hunt for a place to hold church. We park beside the scrub, scramble down the bank, and dip our toes into the stream. We decide to stay; Jesus would have had church here, too.

But first, we play. We splash and make castles in the mud. Jacqueline crouches close to the water and explores all the possibilities. She scoops the soft soil with her fingers and plops piles of it around her. The mud slides down her arms and creeps up her legs; she is oblivious.

"Who wants to pray?" asks Steve, our designated leader, as he begins the call to his disheveled congregation. Jacqueline raises her hand and hears her name. "OK, Jacqui. Go ahead."

I watch her now with a mother's eyes. Hopefully, she'll talk clearly and slowly. It's OK. She's young. Then she stretches out her tiny hands and preaches a sermon with her simple move.

Our daughter bends toward the river and rinses off the dirt. Palms down, she ruffles them in the water. Then tiny fingers fold up and squeeze each other tight.

I do not hear her pray; I do not know if others do. Instead, my mind replays her river wash. She could not pray with dirty hands, could not fold filth between her palms. First, she must let the grime go. Instinctively, she knows the dirt must be washed away before she can pray.

Often, I choose to come to Him with dirty hands. Regularly, I pour out prayers with smears on my soul, unaware that first I need a river wash. He is the Living Water, willing to wash my grime away. Only four, she taught me well this day.

HIDE OUT

"Therefore let everyone who is godly offer prayer to you at a time when you may be found; surely in the rush of great waters they shall not reach him."
(Psalm 32:6)

In our modern world, the rush of great waters threatens. That same overwhelming rush was part and parcel of the lives of the great men and women who walked the earth before us. We hold the misconception that somehow they glided over the top of tumultuous waves, immune from their threatening force and devastation. We are wrong in that belief.

Sequestered in a rotten jail, Joseph knew the choke hold of injustice; the three Hebrew men heaved into a blazing furnace understood the horror of hatred unleashed against them. The patriarch Moses trudged through the desert with millions whining in his ears and complaining every chance they had. Elijah the prophet competed against 300 pagan priests for bragging rights; Jacob was unjustly tricked and denied the wife he'd worked seven years to gain. In a foreign land among strangers, Ruth knew the humiliation of utter poverty in a culture that demeaned widowhood; stolen from her secure home, Esther was placed in the precarious position of being up for grabs by a ruthless pagan king.

King David made note of how God's servants survived and even thrived in their circumstances: "You are a hiding place for me; you preserve me from trouble; you surround me with shouts of deliverance" (Psalm 32:7) These ancient men and women hid themselves within the safety of Jehovah's protection and clung to the truth that he would preserve and rescue them in his perfect time.

These examples from the past whisper hope to our troubled hearts today. With one voice, they direct our attention to the Living God, who promises, "I will instruct you and teach you in the way you should go; I will counsel you with my eye upon you" (Psalm 32:8).

Go ahead, dearest Lord; keep your eye fixed on us, and surround us with your strong arms of deliverance, even today — especially today.

FULL ATTENTION

"Let those who delight in my righteousness shout
for joy and be glad and say evermore, 'Great is the
LORD who delights in the welfare of his servant!'"
(Psalm 35:27)

Weighed down by afternoon heaviness, I am conscious of the rumblings of my volcanic heart where hot lava spurts, smoke spreads, and dust descends in a hazy gloom.

Wounds within seep out in myriad ways; no one truly comprehends my ache but you. I shove them toward you; every one, you soothe and cleanse. Precious friend with gashes in your hands and side, you do not stick bandages on broken places.

You oversee and orchestrate all worlds visible to my naked eye and those beyond my shortsighted vision. You promise peace, and I hasten toward the sound of your voice in written Word. The rest I long for hovers in the background, entering for brief spells, retreating, eluding me. Fears gnaw like menacing mice, bite by bite.

Like that courageous shepherd boy turned warrior-king I plead, "Contend, O Lord, with those who contend with me; fight against those who fight against me!

Take hold of shield and buckler and rise for my help! Draw the spear and javelin against my pursuers! Say to my soul, 'I am your salvation!" (Psalm 35:1-3)

Sing over me as you promise; capture my full attention; submerge my troubled thinking with your strong and certain gaze. Dragon-slayer that you are, brandish sword and spear, and conquer the restless stirrings in my complex heart.

BARRELING DOWN

"Bear one another's burdens, and so fulfill the law of Christ"
(Galatians 6:2).

Sometimes ordinary acts remind of us of heroic ones, and sometimes simple choices illuminate profound truths as satisfying as a splash of cool water on a sun-drenched day.

When our eldest son Bill purchased his first home, every room begged two coats of paint. Within a few hours of calling Greg at law school, our second son was barreling five hours down the highway to provide assistance, leaving behind his own responsibilities and concerns to ensure that his brother had the help he needed.

My heart was full of joy as I pictured our boys working together to accomplish a necessary task. The job was too cumbersome for Bill to tackle alone so Greg willingly jumped into the fray.

Is it any wonder that our Father calls us to minister to one another, to bear burdens, to carry loads too heavy to bear alone? His Father's heart applauds each time we put aside our own concerns and mount up to provide strength, comfort, or practical assistance to our brothers and sisters in the body of Christ. We give our Heavenly Father pleasure when we act compassionately and lovingly serve those he has knitted together as his children.

It's fitting that Christ showed us what perfect brotherly love looks like in the first place. Knowing we carried the burden of sin on our backs, recognizing that by our own efforts we could do nothing to fulfill the righteous requirements of the law, he came barreling down the highway of time and space to offer us eternal assistance. Surrendering his own will, he laid down his life on behalf of all men and women, making a perfect way for us to be forgiven and restored as his brothers and sisters.

Christ is "a brother born for adversity" who calls to us each day, "Come to me, all you who labor and are heavy laden, and I will give you rest. Take my yoke upon you, and learn from me, for I am gentle and lowly in heart, and you will find rest for your souls" (Matthew 11:28).

Calvary made us family with Jesus. Redemption for our souls is what our Brother provided for us all on his own.

REST STOP

"Come away by yourselves...."
(Mark 6:30)

Squeezed between the horrific beheading of John the Baptist and the magnificent miracle of the five thousand stands an overlooked passage that invites us to love Jesus more deeply. Mark 6:30 reads, "The apostles returned to Jesus and told him all that they had done and taught. And he said to them, 'Come away by yourselves to a desolate place and rest a while.'"

Christ listened to the apostles as they shared their struggles and recounted their adventures. The one who unfolded powerful truths, who preached with passion about the Kingdom of Heaven and healed the multitudes at his feet, also gave attention to his friends. He had sent them on a mission; they were relaying their accomplishments. He ceased all other activity and heard what they had to say.

They must have been elated, enthusiastic, and also a bit exhausted. After listening, he demonstrated his love for them in as tender an act as washing the grime from their feet with his own sacred hands. Rather than propelling them out for further ministry, he responded, "Come away. Let's go and rest. I think you need that right now."

The clear image of his acknowledging their weariness gives us a glimpse into the heart of our Savior. When we approach him to relate where we have been and what we have been attempting, he turns his ear in our direction as well. And when we have been occupied with the Father's work, he is mindful that what we need is not another task but time away for rest. We are instructed to listen for his voice. It's reassuring to realize he listens to ours as well.

CARRIER

*"The LORD your God who goes before you will himself
fight for you, just as he did for you in Egypt before
your eyes, and in the wilderness, where you have
seen how the LORD your God carried you, as a man
carries his son, all the way that you went...."*
(Deuteronomy 1:30-31)

Pictures portray a thousand words, and vivid images breathe oxygen into black print on onionskin paper. Moses' description of God in Deutcronomy allows us to peer through a lens and into the heart of our Father in heaven. Where we least expect to find a breathtaking photograph, the verses expose our eyes to the transformational beauty of the living Word in living color. Here we see Jehovah, the High and Holy King, as a most tender parent lovingly embracing his Son.

Not only does the Lord go before his people, not only does he fight for them himself rather than sending an underling to do his bidding, but he also meets the needs of his beloved children the way a protective father cradles a son against his chest. His strong arms form a supportive framework where the child can rest, nestled within the grasp of a Father who would never let go or grow weary of the task at hand. "Just as he did for you in Egypt," he will repeat as often as necessary. He has proven himself trustworthy before and is incapable of inadequacies or inconsistencies of any kind.

When our minds limp with blurry recall and our hearts forget the past goodness of the Lord, flip to the pages we seldom roam to in Scripture. Gaze a moment longer at the Father's image imprinted there. Allow his strength to carry you as far as he wants you to go.

BACKYARD PULPIT

"Preserve me, O God, for in you I take refuge."
(Psalm 16:1)

The racket emanating from my backyard escalated, forcing me to discover what animals could possibly be creating such uproar. With the rumbling sounds of thunder in the background, I peered through the light rainfall and noticed a creamy-brown duck marching back and forth barking orders like a general empowering her troops.

The mesh enclosure surrounding the pool barricaded this mother Gadwall from her four ducklings as they swam frantically in the chlorinated water. The booming summer storm had thrown them off course, and now the newborn ducklings were incapable of maneuvering their way out.

With deafening honks usually associated with 18-wheelers attempting to avoid a head-on collision, this agitated two-pound bird was evidently convinced her brood was in harm's way. Clearly, it was her duty to reassure them at the top of her lungs that even though they were temporarily separated, she would definitely ensure their freedom and reconcile them to her side in prompt fashion.

I eased the enclosure open, she charged in, and they tucked their tiny bodies against hers. Like an Olympic gymnast, she repeatedly propelled herself over the tiled wall, encouraging them to emulate her move and escape their watery prison. Not for one moment did she take a break; the blaring directions and vault maneuvers continued for over an hour. When three of them hurdled out safely, leaving one behind, she kept up the barrage of quacking, squawking, and flapping until the last one finally followed suit.

In this parent's relentless pursuit of her ducklings, in her unceasing directives, in her determined passion to protect and preserve her own, I saw the Lord's own hand. He calls to us through his Word, propelling us to safety by the wisdom and guidance of his Spirit. By his own sacrificial example, he illustrates how to do life well, how to manage and cope and flourish regardless of the hurdles in front or the deep holes beneath. The tiny birds knew they would be rescued. Their job was to listen, follow, and obey.

Hopefully, this big truth from a minute bird that preached her heart out from a backyard pulpit will not disappear any time soon.

ALONGSIDE

"May the LORD answer you in the day of trouble!
May the name of the God of Jacob protect you!"
(Psalm 20:1)

On occasion, even sovereigns slip off crowns and don battle garb; regal wear is not suited for wrestling in wartime.

David bows before the Lord and begs help, conscious that his title topples before the tyrants arrayed against him. Conscious of the pressing needs, David invites priest and people to storm heaven on his behalf. "May he send you help from the sanctuary and give you support from Zion...may he grant you your heart's desire and fulfill all your plans," (Psalm 20:2,4) they cry to God in unison for their beloved king.

No throne in sight, but troubles still thrust their ugly heads inside our common world. We, too, wage war and require protection from visible foes and invisible forces. Our advanced, computer-savvy chariots and 21st-century warhorses still quiver and buckle before the attack at hand. Who will help us maneuver through the onslaught? Who will fight for us?

We hear reports from battlefields in distant lands that friends must now withstand enemy advances. As the news filters through, we shudder and then recognize we are capable of brandishing weaponry in their defense. Like David's gathering we storm heaven with our cries: "Jehovah, answer us in this day of trouble with the saving might of your right hand. May the name of the God of Jacob protect him as he fights leukemia; uphold her as she buckles beneath the weight of anxiety; comfort them as they cower with grief; strengthen her to face her son's imprisonment; give courage to fight the stronghold of his addiction."

Kings and commoners alike desperately depend on warriors on the sidelines who courageously join in the battle by entreating Almighty God on their behalf. Our roles are vital to the outcome of the clash. May we keep lifting those we love before the High King no matter how long their "day of trouble" lasts.

PART III

HIS PERFECT WAY

"Jesus said to him, 'I am the way...'"
John 14:6

HANDS-ON

"How are such mighty works done by his hands?"
(Mark 6:2c)

H is calloused hands – accustomed to hammer and nails, splinters of wood and planks of lumber – carted carpentry tools long before they healed a child, touched a leper, or broke bread to nourish a crowd. The carpenter from Nazareth who created the world from nothing would one day be stretched out on a crude wooden beam for men's salvation. But first, he handled and marked his world with enormous touches of love.

His voice spoke the earth into existence as his words alone cast galaxies abroad, all of it good. But, when he rubbed shoulders with humanity, when his eyes beheld the wounded and the lame, his hands reached out to transform what was not good at all.

Though the disciples adamantly disagreed, Jesus leaned forward to hold the babies. "Let the children come to me, and do not hinder them," he cried. The busy Master, with pressure mounting on all sides, took time to touch the little ones brought to him. He embraced them and blessed them, because they were significant in his eyes (Mark 10:13-16). He expelled evil spirits from a young boy whose father had come begging for deliverance. After the spirits departed, the boy lay like a corpse. "But Jesus took him by the hand and lifted him up, and he arose" (Mark 9:27). Taking, lifting, rising; evil was made to flee before the force of God.

When he arrived in Bethsaida, a blind man's friends implored Jesus to heal him. The Gospel declares that he took the man by the hand, walked him outside the village, moistened his eyes with saliva, and "laid his hands on him." When Christ placed his fingers on the blinded eyes a second time, "his sight was restored, and he saw every-thing clearly" (Mark 8:23,35).

Those same hands would later lift the cup of the new covenant, would clutch the ground in Gethsemane, and would haul the cross to Calvary. Those hands still wait to bring us aid, soothe our grief, strengthen our weakness, and fill up our gaping holes.

Our hand in his...his hands on us. Hold us, dear Savior, broken and splintered though we are.

DIRECTIONS

"And the disciples did as Jesus had directed
them, and they prepared the Passover."
(Matthew 26:19)

They often got it wrong. Jesus' band of followers usually ended up making poor choices, succumbing to sleepiness when he desperately needed companionship, running away like frightened mice when he could have used a little lion-hearted friendship.

His time had come, and it seemed everyone was eagerly plotting his demise. The chief priests, the elders of the people, and the high priest were all concocting devious plans to arrest and kill Jesus.[51] Greedy Judas rubbed his grubby paws together and probed, "What will you give me if I deliver him over to you?" (Matthew 26:15).

In their midst, Jesus' closest friends wisely obeyed his simple instructions for preparing the Passover. At least this time they got it right.

He loved them regardless. He was on their side when they followed his directions and ensured their last meal together was a success, and he loved them unconditionally when they tucked their garments between their knees and deserted him, abandoning him to face the enemy alone.

Wanting to prepare them for the tumultuous events that lay ahead, he warned, "You will all fall away because of me this night" (Matthew 26:31). In a rousing chorus, they vowed to die rather than betray him. Yet, he knew their hearts, knew they were weak, and understood implicitly that they would not withstand the pressure.

Because his love was rooted in forgiveness, he reminded them that after it all went awry he would meet back up with them in Galilee. He did not scold or rebuke them for their frailty. Jesus understood that their fears would paralyze them, ensnaring the Galilean fishermen, transforming their muscles to mush. The Shepherd's sacrificial devotion would triumph even while the sheep scattered from the blow.

On occasion, disciples will get it all wrong. Sometimes we follow the Master perfectly. Always, he loves us graciously, showers us with mercy, forgives our deficiencies, and calls us to continue the journey faithfully, our feet following the path he chose all those years ago.

HIGHWAY

"And Peter directed his gaze at him, as
did John, and said, 'Look at us.'"
(Acts 3:4)

At first glance, the story doesn't seem thrilling. The man is lame; the disciples show up; the man is healed. No big deal. Jesus did it all the time. On closer inspection, when we read through the Acts 3 account again and then scrutinize it further, parallel truths somersault off the page like trapeze artists in midair.

The lame man sees Peter and John approaching the temple and begs them for money. They refuse. Instead, Peter offers him these profound words: "I have no silver or gold, but what I do have I give to you. In the name of Jesus Christ of Nazareth, rise up and walk."

The Father's plan reverberates through this phrase. In the way the apostles gaze at the physically lame man, God gazes at us and sees our spiritual disfigurement. The disciples initiate the cripple's healing without him requesting it; God has initiated our healing from sin. Salvation has been his idea all along.

Peter and John could throw a few coins in the man's hand and keep walking. But, because they've learned the Master's ways, they see the beggar's greater need and heal him in the name of Jesus Christ.

Our Heavenly Father has always recognized the true need of mankind and never dispatches trivial solutions. From the manger in Bethlehem to the empty tomb, God stoops toward the world paralyzed by sin and declares, "Look at me. What I do have I give to you. In the name of Jesus Christ of Nazareth, rise up and LIVE."

That's truth enough for us to leap with joy.

ON OUR SIDE

"He who did not spare his own Son but
gave him up for us all...."
(Romans 8:32)

We've all had them: those days when a bonus was promised, but bills arrived instead; times when leaky roofs, court summons, and solemn physicians showed their unexpected faces; seasons when it appeared everything was against us.

Paul the apostle could relate. His bad days more closely resembled wretched events for routine beatings, jail time, and shipwrecks were the norm. In Acts 25, we find him awaiting release after two years of being confined to prison. The first eight verses of the chapter tell us that the chief priest, the prominent men, the Jews, and the governor were all bringing charges and laying out a case "against" him.

Clearly, regardless of who assaulted him, God was his solid reinforcement. No court, king, or council could stack up enough false evidence or witnesses to shut him down. God even ensured that the powerful empire of Rome would protect Paul from all harm. This servant had kingdom work to accomplish; no one and nothing could interrupt this plan.

When Paul penned the book of Romans, he dramatically declared, "If God is for us, who can be against us? He who did not spare his own Son, but gave him up for us all, how will he not also with him graciously give us all things?" (Romans 8:31)

Our unchanging God stands with us, too. He is for us in every part of the raging battle. Jesus hanging on the cross, Jesus emerging from the tomb, Jesus living within us today – these provide proof positive that God Almighty keeps his word. Who or what can possibly be against us when all of heaven is on our side?

CANOPY

"They were all amazed and glorified God,
saying, 'We never saw anything like this!'"
(Mark 2:12)

We enjoy packaging God in manageable proportions: a single serving of Deity, not too much to overindulge our spiritual palate. If he is just the right size, then we fit him into our day in the appropriate places and banish him to the sidelines at our discretion.

It is easier to tolerate God when he doesn't meddle in our affairs and demand what we cannot deliver. We like God to be within range to answer our pleas for help but not so near as to cramp our own particular lifestyle.

A casual reading of the gospels may allow us to stroll beneath the canopy of this erroneous thinking for a time. How kind of him, to cast out demons and make diseases flee. How thoughtful, that he would feed the multitudes with little more than a bag lunch. Inspiring that he saw potential in fishermen and lounged comfortably with tax collectors and various sordid specimens of humanity. How pleasant that he was always interested in teaching and proclaiming truth. This Jesus was certainly a model citizen.

Yet when we prolong our trek through Scripture, when we meditate and contemplate the familiar stories and statements, we quickly realize that Christ defies trivializing. He invites serious thought and cannot be easily dismissed.

In the opening verses of the gospel of Mark, the spotlight is definitely on the person of Jesus Christ. We encounter him proclaiming, speaking, calling, asking, initiating, controlling, and displaying his all-encompassing authority. He invites his hearers to repent, believe, and follow him. He mesmerizes his audience; he silences demons with a few pointed words. Christ heals those sick in the flesh and those infested with evil spirits, without ever seeming out of breath or out of control.

The truth is, the Man must be reckoned with. We must come to grips with his deity, for he is completely and divinely beyond our comprehension.

In fact, we are the ones in desperate need of being managed by him.

COMPLETELY DONE

"And you, who were dead in your trespasses and the
uncircumcision of your flesh, God made alive together with
him, having forgiven us all our trespasses, by canceling
the record of debt that stood against us with its legal
demands. This he set aside, nailing it to the cross."
(Colossians 2:13-14)

When Jesus rebuked the unclean spirit of a young boy, when he broke the chains of death that bound Jairus' daughter, and when he restored a man's withered hand in the middle of an ordinary Sabbath gathering, no one assisted him in the healing process. By Christ's distinct power, might, and majesty, the evil spirit cowered and fled, the girl rose from her deathbed, and the crippled man was made whole again.

In all four Gospels, whenever Jesus healed, a perfect healing occurred. The sick, the lame, and the tortured soul all left his presence transformed and utterly whole. No paralytic ever limped away after Jesus cured his palsy; no leper had leftover blemishes disfiguring his skin; no physician or therapist was called to complete the half-done miracle.

Likewise, when Jesus heals us spiritually by washing away our sins, forgiving our transgressions, and erasing our debts, our healing is also absolutely complete.

All by himself, Jesus forgives, cleanses, and redeems; no one needs to assist him with his saving grace.

The mentality that asserts, "God helps those who help themselves," mistakenly believes that we must participate to ensure salvation works. Surely, our good deeds, righteous acts, or some legalistic addition is a necessary requirement.

However Christ doesn't need our help any more than he needed the blind man's assistance in restoring his sight. Jesus forgives all our transgressions, cancels the entire debt, and nails all our sins to the cross. Though we were spiritually dead and enslaved in a kingdom of darkness, he rescued us and gave us new life, forevermore.

It's perfectly fitting, then, for Peter to proclaim, "And there is salvation in no one else, for there is no other name under heaven given among men by which we must be saved" (Acts 4:12). That thought all by itself should remind us that we are forgiven entirely, that our debt is cancelled completely, and that every legal demand has been met perfectly by the Savior of the World.

OBSCURE SCENES

"Peace to you, do not be afraid. Your God and the God
of your father has put treasure in your sacks for you."
(Genesis 43:23)

Scattered across the Epistles the phrase "grace and mercy" appear as inseparable vines twisted around the solid trunk of Scripture.

These concepts did not first sprout from the blood-soaked earth beneath the cross. The roots of these two words run deep, beginning with the grand story of Creation. We first learn about grace and mercy when God covered the shame of Adam and Eve with a slain animal's coat in that intimate exchange in the garden.

Because our Father is consistent and unchanging, his passionate love for his people cannot be disguised. He reveals his uncompromising nature in obscure scenes and in recognizable passages, unveiling his endless, redeeming love.

In the familiar story of Joseph in Genesis 43, the brothers return to Egypt a second time to beg bread from the very one they sold into slavery years before.

Joseph is unfamiliar in his stately attire, his Egyptian tongue and appearance masking his Hebrew origin. Each time the sons of Israel prostrate themselves before Joseph they fulfill his dream, but they cannot erase the thirteen years they stole or the anguish their evil hearts forced him to endure.

Joseph has every right to hate his brothers, and he has the powerful Egyptian forces at his disposal to unleash the cruelest forms of revenge. When the ten treacherous brothers show up on his prestigious governmental doorstep, it would be a mere trifle to order them dragged away, and executed. Nobody would have ever known where those starving Hebrews ended. Who would fault him for measuring back punishment in equal measure?

Instead, a picture of God's grace emerges when Joseph has the grain bags on each brother's donkey filled the first time, and filled again, with their money returned in full. Rather than throwing them in well-deserved iron chains and casting them into a dimly lit, rat-infested dungeon, he speaks with them, invites them into his own home, and lays food before them from his own table.

In Joseph's response, we get a taste of God's brand of forgiveness. Mercy is God withholding the punishment we rightly deserve. Grace is God's abundant provision, which we are totally incapable of securing for ourselves. Joseph, as a type of Christ, reflects both these gifts to his undeserving family.

On the cross our beloved Savior freely poured out grace and mercy abundantly from the storehouse of the Father's love. Our sacred Brother endured the greatest humiliation and chained himself to our sins to be in the perfect position to free us and forgive us forever.

MISS THE MARK

*"In vain do they worship me, teaching as
doctrines the commandments of men."*
(Mark 7:7)

H e mingled easily with the mongrels of his day and the wom-
en who sold their bodies after selling their souls. Perfectly
at ease in their presence, willing to share a meal or a deep
slice of conversation, Christ drew them like beggars to bread. The
Teacher who healed, the Prophet who listened, the Messiah who
served, he welcomed them even while they were aware that their
sin-soaked garments brushed against holiness.

Calling children to his side for blessings, he cradled these less-
than-desirable members of society and reprimanded his followers
who demanded they depart. The King had absolute patience and
limitless time for every unwanted waif and leper who approached.
Why, then, did one specific group of people infuriate him immense-
ly, causing him to lash them with stinging words as sharp as the whip
he would later use to cleanse the temple?

Christ unleashed his harshest condemnation on the Pharisees.
Repeatedly, he chastised them, labeling these scoundrels "hypocrites." Mark 7 captures one such lashing: "This people honors me
with their lips, but their heart is far from me...You have a fine way

of rejecting the commandment of God in order to establish your tradition."

Matthew 23:13 spells out clearly why they exasperated him. "For you shut the kingdom of heaven in people's faces. For you neither enter yourselves nor allow those who would enter to go in." Consumed with the external, the Pharisees totally missed the eternal God standing before them. They were busy cleansing hands and dishes without ever taking thought that their souls desperately needed a washing. Christ wanted them to realize, "The heart is deceitful about all things, and desperately sick, who can understand it?" (Jeremiah 17:9) He knew clearly the wretched condition of man's heart, and that outward cleansing could never purify it.

Each morning he awoke with the realization that the cost of cleansing the heart was high indeed; his blood would be extracted in the process. Saving humanity would entail thorns on his brow, flogging to his back, nails in his hands, fists to his face, a spear to his side, and an unbearable cross. Is it any wonder that the Pharisees' attention to outward cleansing as a means of pleasing God caused him dismay?

Occupied with minutia, they completely missed the Messiah. May we not imitate their stubborn heart and foolish ways.

WAITING IN LINE

"When he went ashore he saw a great crowd,
and he had compassion on them because they
were like sheep without a shepherd."
(Mark 6:34)

Compassion is not a flimsy garment slung across the Savior's shoulders; this attribute is woven through the perfect fabric of his being.

When unwelcomed crowds surged forward, disrupting his vacation plans for the weary disciples, he did not recoil from their demands. He viewed this mass of humanity with eyes of love and willingly interrupted his schedule for them. These "sheep without a shepherd" ran straight toward his tender heart.

Since the disciples did not yet comprehend Kingdom behavior, they were eager for Christ to dismiss the throng to scrounge on their own. But his intrinsic kindness would not allow this solution, and he declared, "Let's feed them all! What do we have on hand?" Presented with a boy's puny lunch, his power allowed for every sheep to graze extravagantly. He looked to heaven, blessed the bread, broke it apart, and gave it to the disciples to "set before the people" (Mark 6:42).

The verse ends with a succinct description of our Lord: "And he divided the two fish among them all." All by itself, this one line is a brilliant definition of Christ. The Master took a handful of food and multiplied it miraculously, feeding over 5,000 hungry individuals at a God-sized feast. His compassion made him acutely aware they had aching bellies needing to be filled; his power enabled him to satisfy their hunger thoroughly.

He hasn't changed; he never will. Compassion took him all the way to the cross. His power took him all the way out of the tomb. Wait awhile for him to dress you with his uncompromising strength and tenderness.

BY THE SEASHORE

*"And he was teaching them many things in parables,
and in his teaching he said to them: 'Listen!'"*
(Mark 4:2)

The situation could easily have turned ugly.

As the crowds surged toward him, they threatened to crush Christ with their aggressive behavior. The wind whipped waves and slapped them along the shoreline; he calmly maneuvered into the safety of the vessel he had requested his disciples to prepare. The boat bobbed in rhythm with the water as the disciples anchored close to shore. With the lake to his back and the multitudes perched before him, the Master Teacher projected his voice, positioning himself in order for the crowd to hear every word.

In sandals covered in sand and garments splashed by Galilee's sea, the people pressed against the water's edge for another helping of what this Healer had previously delivered. The leper, the paralytic, and the one who now boasted an un- shriveled hand were effective advertisements of his miraculous touch. The silenced demons spoke volumes, too. Where disorderly conduct could have reigned, they were held spellbound by this King holding court within the confines of a simple wooden boat. No royal throne had ever held such distinction as when he extended truth to them like a regal scepter.

"Listen," was the first word from the teacher's lips. Before he even began the parable of the sower and the seeds, before he explained the significance of the soils, the Rabbi seized their attention with his supreme authority.

"Listen to the words I am going to share, though words are strewn generously on every shore and field. Quiet your hearts; otherwise, you will not be able to hear the truth I want to give." The Master Storyteller soothed the crowds then; he still longs to quiet our restless souls.

He will bring order to our disheveled world, calm to our chaos, as we wait attentively for him to speak by the shore of our own windswept Galilee.

PIVOTAL

"Rejoice in hope, be patient in tribulation,
be constant in prayer."
(Romans 12:12)

T he disciples could have scattered in a dozen directions after Christ ascended to heaven. Yet, as an act of obedience, they listened to Jesus' final instructions to return to Jerusalem until they were "clothed with power from on high" (Luke 24:49b). Huddled in that upper room, waiting for the Holy Spirit's entrance, they were consumed with an important activity. What kept these men enthralled at a time like this?

Rather than mulling over the incredible events that had unfolded between the crucifixion and the Lord's ascension or figuring out what would occur next, they were knee-deep in prayer. After listing each of the eleven disciples' names, Acts 1:14 tells us, "All these with one accord were devoting themselves to prayer...."

This was probably a perfect time to panic, but they chose instead to use their time perfectly. A new disciple had to be selected to replace Judas, and the apostles knew prayer was the key component for such a critical decision.

Christ had modeled this precisely. From Luke we learn, "In these days he went out to the mountain to pray, and all night he continued in prayer to God. And when day came, he called his disciples and chose from them twelve, whom he named apostles" (Luke 6:12-13). Before Jesus had made the pivotal selection of the twelve, he had devoted himself to prayer. The apostles followed suit.

As disciples of the Lord Jesus, when we face decisions in the major or minor categories, shouldn't we imitate Christ, too?

OVER THE TOP

"You therefore must be perfect, as your
heavenly Father is perfect."
(Matthew 5:48)

An impossible command dangles off the end of Matthew 5 like a daunting challenge. Jesus calls us to the highest of standards, requiring us to be as perfect as our Father in Heaven. What an outrageous claim to make to frail humanity. Who could ever fulfill such an outlandish demand?

Standing within the hallowed corridors of the Sermon on the Mount, Jesus' most familiar discourse, this call to perfection is startling. We are forced to recognize that this requirement is as much beyond us as fingering the Milky Way. Of course, we strive to be meek and merciful, as the Beatitudes strongly suggest.

Naturally, in the verses leading up to this one, we attempt to be the salt of the earth, the light of the world, or a brilliant city situated on a hill. But to measure up to God Almighty himself is altogether unfeasible.

Jesus would agree. Knowing we could not, he has gone ahead of us and done it all. Throughout the three chapters that make up the sermon, we understand that everything the Lord calls us to obey, he has accomplished first. Blessed are the meek, the merciful, and the peacemakers, Jesus teaches. He puts the words in front of us but first fleshes them out with his life.

He illustrates meekness every time his supernatural strength is under control. Mercy run through his veins and gushes out on the lepers he touches, the widows he comforts, the lame who dance away from his presence. His entire mission on planet earth is to restore peace, reconciling God with flawed humanity.

His sermon asks us to do our good works primarily to bring glory to the Father, and he demonstrates this principle continuously before the crowds as "they glorified God, who had given such authority to men" (Matthew 9:8).

"Love your enemies and pray for those who persecute you," the Lord says. "Forgive others their trespasses," he advises, going on to demonstrate these attributes as he hangs dying on the cross with his tormentors gambling for his garments close to his bloodied feet. "Father, forgive them, for they know not what they do," he prays, living out sacrificial love right before their eyes.

Hide away in secret when you pray, and do not practice your righteousness to receive man's praise. What he has commanded, he has fulfilled. Our Lord steals away to the backside of mountaintops to pray, performs his miracles in obscure villages away from the maddening crowds, and begs most of those he heals to keep the miracle quiet.

Do not be anxious for any part of your life, Jesus challenges us, but seek God's kingdom first. Christ wakes each morning fully aware of the crucifixion in store, but he never allows this oncoming freight train to distract him from his all-consuming mission of bringing the Kingdom of God to earth. Just as he promises, Christ fulfills every single portion of the law (Matthew 5:17). Every command he lays out for us, he has first lived out for us. Knowing we could never fulfill the requirements of the law, he has accomplished what was impossible for us to obtain.

Christ takes on our sin and gives us his righteousness. In the Father's eyes, we are perfect; the blameless Lamb of God has made that absolutely certain. May we never get over the perfect wonder of it all!

TRACK RECORD

"Repent therefore, and turn again, that your
sins may be blotted out, that times of refreshing
may come from the presence of the Lord..."
(Acts 3:19-20a)

We trip awkwardly, sprawling our secret sins in full view of cynical eyes. Later, we cringe, fearful of lifting our heads lest anyone condemn us further for our regretful behavior. Ashamed, we bury our faces in self-condemnation. Who will forgive us now? Who will refurbish our shameful lives?

God will. If we doubt his ability to forgive and restore, if we believe our transgressions beyond his redemption, we fail to comprehend his track record.

In Acts 3, Peter teaches us the radical extent of God's forgiveness. A crowd of Jews in Solomon's portico of the temple surrounds the apostle. Boldly, Peter lays out God's case against them, reminding them they were the ones who delivered Jesus to Pilate. He tells them plainly that they denied the Holy and Righteous One and actually killed the Author of life (Acts 3:13-15).

Yet even these criminal acts against the Son of God do not disqualify them from God's forgiveness. Further in the chapter, Peter reassures them that they "acted in ignorance" and calls them to repentance, to make Jesus Christ their Lord.

Through the lips of Peter, God actually extended forgiveness to the ones who participated in Jesus' death. What iniquity could be more heinous? Since God willingly forgave these wretched offenders, we can be certain he is willing to forgive us as well. Our complete reconciliation with the Father is possible. Ask him to pardon and restore us to fellowship with him. His Son already paid the full price for us to obtain that costly gift.

BOULDER

*"And they were saying to one another, 'Who will roll
away the stone for us from the entrance of the tomb?'"*
(Mark 16:3)

The spices weighed heavily in their arms; one thought was heaviest on their minds. The women had the strongest desire to anoint the body of their Lord, but they were far too weak to heave away the enormous stone blocking the entrance of the tomb. Who could possibly move the boulder for them to accomplish this important task?

God already had; they were simply unaware. Mark tells us the women came early on the first day of the week, when the sun had risen. They had not yet discovered that the *Son* had also risen and was no longer in need of burial spices.

We are often similar to those friends of Jesus. We bring our troubling questions to the Lord, wringing our hands in earnest, uncertain of how to solve the particular problem blocking our view.

Unbeknownst to us, the Resurrected Lord has already taken care of the situation. With the power that raised him from the dead, he is confronting our seemingly overwhelming circumstances and is providing a solution even while we are wondering exactly what to do. *Who will care for me in my old age? Who will sustain me during this financial down turn? Who will help me bear this loss? Who will provide me wisdom to know which way to go?*

He will. He has. He can. He does. Some questions simply were answered a very long time ago.

WHOLE WAY

"Moved with pity, he stretched out his hand and
touched him and said to him, 'I will; be clean.'"
(Mark 1:41)

The ghastly label of leper was his sole identification, for we are not privy to his name or the city of his origin. Banished from society, his kind would not presume to scale the lowest rung of the crudest ladder of that day.

Whisperings about the Christ who commanded evil spirits to obey and diseases to evaporate had filtered through the streets, down the alleyways, and slipped inside the cracks of the leprosy barracks where he hid. All the sick brought to Jesus' doorway in Capernaum were healed (Mark 1:33-34). Surely, there was room for one more.

With the heroic courage of a warrior fighting for his own existence, the leper bent his knees and begged, "If you will, you can make me clean" (Mark 1:40). I know what you are capable of; I grasp the fact that you do the impossible, but I am uncertain if I am even worthy of your power."

Three of the Gospels distinctly record that Christ, "stretched out his hand and touched him." Before cleansing his diseased skin, the all-compassionate Savior healed the scars inside the man left from his years of imprisonment within the confines of leprosy. The Great

Physician is the Good Shepherd who carries lambs close to his heart, even the blemished ones no one else considers valuable.

The God we serve sees beyond our seeping wounds and never recoils from our imperfections. Our staggering loads never stump the Savior. His powerful hands are capable of handling them; his tender heart moves to make us whole.

HOVERING

"They are darkened in their understanding, alienated
from the life of God because of the ignorance that
is in them, due to their hardness of heart."
(Ephesians 4:18)

They scrutinized Jesus like a hawk peering at its prey, intent on swooping in swiftly and gobbling him alive. It was the Sabbath, and a man with a deformed hand stood timidly in the synagogue; the religious elite dared Jesus to make a move.

Their veins pulsed with loathing for the Healer, and their silence smacked of accusations and resentment. Jesus beckoned to the man with the withered hand and offered the sulking ones a proposal: "Is it lawful on the Sabbath to do good or to do harm, to save life or to kill?" (Mark 3:4)

The Master Questioner stilled their lethal tongues, but their arrogant indifference and wickedness stirred him to anger. In fact, the Gospel writer records that Jesus took the time to look directly at them, to peer into their hardened hearts. The reflection "grieved" him deeply.

The skeptics could not intimidate the Savior, and their lack of compassion didn't prevent him from accomplishing his will. Christ did not move a muscle to bring about the healing. He restored the man simply by speaking four words, — "Stretch out your hand," failing to break any Sabbath regulations.

Immediately after the healing they swarmed outside, menacing birds of prey hovering to destroy the Miracle-maker, the gentle Healer, the Savior of the world.

His enemies would succeed temporarily. Jesus would hang on a cross, and they would foolishly suppose their mission accomplished as his blood dripped to the ground. They stood inches away from Jesus, and yet never heard him calling them to "Come." Preoccupied with plotting his demise, they failed miserably at preventing his greatest act of "doing good" as he saved mankind from sin's withering hold.

Consumed with doing him harm, they totally missed the Savior who came to rescue us from crippled hearts and stony souls.

Gentle healer, you who see within, do me good this day as I stretch out my withered places to you. With your Words of life and touch of love, restore and renew all the worn-out parts in me you know to be in need.

STRIPES

*"For all have sinned and fall short of the glory
of God, and are justified by his grace as a gift,
through the redemption that is in Christ Jesus."*
(Romans 3:23-24)

At first glance, it appeared there had been a grave mistake. Somehow, the Roman state and the hierarchy of religious Jews had erroneously concluded that Jesus Christ was a criminal. Soldiers swarmed the execution site as he was strung between two undistinguished robbers. Written in three different languages, his charge was positioned above the piercing thorns shoved into his brow. His brutalized body was fixed to wooden beams by hammer and nails, the gruesome execution carried out with tools familiar to the Nazarene carpenter.

All four gospel accounts reveal staggering injustice. How dare they treat the Son of God like a common criminal! He allowed them to bind him with ropes and drag him before Pilate. He refused to defend himself before their accusations and accepted their spittle, fists, and lashings without summoning the legions of angels at his disposal. With utter restraint, the Son of God yielded to treatment as a vicious criminal because he was implicitly aware that a great crime had occurred.

God's holy laws had been violated. This was the crime worthy of excruciating punishment. Ever since Adam and Eve raised their hands in the Garden of Eden and chose contrary to God's commands, mankind had mimicked their rebellion.

The transgressions of men and women through the ages were punishable by Death (Romans 6:23). The penalty had to fit the enormity of the crime.

The only one whose blood was innocent of any failings, the only one who never had to ask forgiveness of another human being or of God Almighty, was the only one capable of shouldering all we deserved. Every offense against God by every human through all of time was transferred to him in agonizing proportions. "The Lord has laid on him the iniquity of us all" (Isaiah 53:6).

Jesus' jail time reconciled us to the Father. He wore the stripes for us to be free to become all he intended us to be.

WELL SPRING

*"So Jesus, wearied as he was from his
journey, was sitting beside the well."
(John 4:6)*

C hrist knew no lack when he ruled from heaven, but while
journeying through Samaria the Creator was thirsty, needy,
wanting. Allowing himself to be dependent on others, shield-
ing his omnipotence, he positioned himself inside of time and space,
accepting our limitations as his own.

His actions demonstrate love on the cross and love spilled out by
the well; thirst on lips that spoke every drop of water into existence;
weariness within the arms of the One who held galaxies in his grasp.

Through him we learn all about sacrificial surrender poured
out by the gallon. Christ never reconsidered when he contemplated
the cost of the manger, or the cross, or the parched path he had to
press through on his journey from one to the other. In contrast, we
grumble at the slightest inconvenience we are called to endure. We
quibble, "Do you really want me to give this up for you? Are you sure
there isn't someone better equipped for this task?"

When Christ asked the Samaritan for a drink, it opened the way
for him to give her himself. Likewise, whatever sacrifice he might
ask of us presents an enormous opportunity for us to experience far

more of the height, depth, and breadth of his unconditional, all-encompassing love. He is Living Water, rushing inside, swirling within our hearts and renewing our minds. When we are tempted to shrink from what lies ahead, let us drink even more deeply of the One who is "a spring of water welling up to eternal life" (John 4:14b).

MOUNTAINTOP

"And when they lifted up their eyes, they
saw no one but Jesus only."
(Matthew 17:8)

e envy them sometimes, the twelve who walked so closely
beside the Savior that they heard the Gospel from his
lips and witnessed the miracles from the frontlines.
They were the Carpenter's nearest companions as he traversed the
Galilean hills and journeyed through the Judean countryside. Yet,
along with their privileged position came hazardous turns with turbulent storms, gardens swarming with Roman guards, and mountaintop experiences overshadowed by ancient prophets and God's own
fearsome voice – reason enough for fear to be a steady companion,
too.

When Peter, James, and John caught sight of Jesus' transfigured
face radiating like the sun, Peter's nervous chatter was suddenly interrupted by Jehovah's dramatic proclamation: "This is my beloved Son,
with whom I am well pleased; listen to him." The disciples buried
their faces in the rocky soil, trembling with the kind of fear that con-
sumes every smidge of courage. Their familiar friend now possessed
a supernatural countenance and prophets long dead were present.

Moreover, Jehovah had taken the opportunity to bestow commendations out loud. Into this scary scenario Jesus demonstrates gentleness kindness. "But Jesus came and touched them, saying, 'Rise, and have no fear.' And when they lifted their eyes, they saw no one but Jesus only" (Matthew 17:7-8).

They retraced their steps down the mountain then, deep in conversation but void of fear. Christ had entered their dread-filled place and with his touch and voice clarified that they had nothing whatsoever to be afraid of.

He speaks a similar message into our troubled days. Like his band of followers, we may become overwhelmed by threatening situations that produce sweaty palms and heart palpitations. We cower and cringe; he speaks and stills. He gives us permission to stand up and recognize that with him by our side we can "Rise, and have no fear."

May we lift up our eyes like that trio on the mountaintop and recognize that Jesus is fully present as our brave companion. The Father instructed them to listen to his Son; that's good advice to follow, no matter the direction we face.

RUNNING THE SHOW

*"This, the first of his signs, Jesus did at Cana
in Galilee, and manifested his glory.
And his disciples believed in him."*
(John 2:11)

Servants are usually background figures, unimportant and un-impressive... except when Jesus is in the picture. Then every-thing changes; the ordinary explodes and the unusual occurs. Take Cana, for instance. Jesus is invited to a wedding with his dis-ciples, and the guests are left without wine. Mary appeals to Jesus to fix the problem and informs the servants, "Do whatever he tells you" (John 2:5).

Amazing events unfold when the servants listen and obey. First, Jesus instructs them to fill the 30-gallon jars with water, then draw some out, and take it to the master of the feast.

Christ never touches the water going into the jugs or the wine coming out of them. He never speaks to the bride, the groom, or the steward in charge of the feast. His words are for the servants only, and the miracle occurs as the servants carry out his precise instructions.

The honored guests are treated to fine wine; the host is applauded for providing the best; but the servants receive the greatest wedding gift. They alone know who has orchestrated the amazing new batch of wine.

The servants who faithfully complete the assigned task have the luxury of front-row seats at the very first miracle Jesus performs. Their lives are forever altered because they experience firsthand the miraculous intervention of the Son of God.

We have the same privilege today. We, too, can listen for his voice as he directs us through the written Word. Our assignments might be ordinary and routine, and our calling might be unappealing to others, but as servants of the Living God we get to participate in Kingdom work every time we show up and obey.

Wine flows from water jugs when Jesus is running the show. Let him.

THE WILDERNESS WAY

"The Spirit immediately drove him out into the wilderness."
(Mark 1:12)

The wilderness appears as wasteland. The weather is scorching, the living conditions exhausting, the nourishment scanty. Weary and haggard, we trudge through, begging desperately for this part of the journey to end quickly.

Perhaps the worst part of the trek is the nagging sense that we are alone; God has abandoned us here because he is angry and is unleashing appropriate punishment. We are unworthy and have brought this accursed situation on ourselves; he is unmindful of our wretched circumstances.

The opening verses of the Gospel of Mark prove that logic as flawed. John the Baptist has just immersed the Lamb of God in the Jordan River; the heavens are torn wide open, and the Holy Spirit descends on Christ in the form of a dove.

The culmination of this dramatic moment in history is the Father's voice booming from the doorway of heaven: "You are my Beloved Son; with you I am well pleased." The highest possible praise bestowed from the King of the Universe on his Beloved Son is the finest form of affirmation and approval.

What happens next? How does the Father top this stunning proclamation? The next two verses tell us that "immediately" God sent Jesus into the wilderness to be tempted by Satan for forty days.

The Father was exceedingly pleased with his Son, and yet he allowed Jesus to enter the gut-wrenching wilderness for a specific reason, for a designated period.

Since we are his children, whom he is consistently transforming into the likeness of his Son, he will also allow us to enter similar situations.

"For it was fitting that he, for whom and by whom all things exist, in bringing many sons to glory, should make the founder of their salvation perfect through suffering" (Hebrews 2:10). The Beloved Son had to endure the wilderness for our sake. When we are made to wander through, he is the perfect guide.

COURSE AHEAD

"Complete my joy by being of the same mind, having the same love, being in full accord and of one mind."
(Philippians 2:2)

S mack dab between confessing Jesus as the Messiah and witnessing Christ's spectacular Transfiguration, Peter treats the Lord as if he is a naughty schoolboy talking out of turn.

Knowing the horrific future in store for him in Jerusalem, Christ begins to prepare his disciples for the onslaught ahead. Because he clearly understands the agony he will have to endure and the ramifications for his followers, Jesus confides in them. Peter does not like the direction Christ is going and scolds him, reprimanding him for daring to utter such nonsensical thoughts about suffering and death.

Simon Peter's words sting Christ like a whip, and he confronts the disciple with startling force. "Get behind me, Satan! You are a hindrance to me" (Matthew 16:23). In a grand summary of Peter's misguided focus, Christ continues to slice through to the source of his friend's faulty words. "For you are not setting your mind on the things of God, but on the things of man."

That phrase illuminates our own thought processes at times. Whenever we misunderstand Christ's actions, when we scold him for not lining up circumstances to our liking, we mimic Peter. When we want to chastise the Lord for our sufferings or for allowing conflicting scenarios in our lives, we are imitating the fisherman's foolishness.

Christ lays out truth and does not ask the disciples to agree with it, understand it, or alter it. He presents it to them as a friend shares intimate details of his life and as the Savior fully aware of the course ahead. It's as if he says to them, "Suffering is bearing down the track toward me and it will soon crush me completely, extinguishing my very life. But, wait. I want to make certain you understand that this is not the end. Be of good cheer. I will rise again."

The risen Savior will always provide the best strategy for the road ahead. May we trust him to direct our course and may we follow his leading to "set our minds" on the things of God and not on the things of man.

TOUR GUIDE

"For he was numbered among us and was
allotted his share in this ministry."
(Acts 1:17)

"Treachery" is a ghastly word. It conjures up images of despicable actions with villainous intent. Judas comes quickly to mind. With a kiss reserved for friendship, he pressed his lips against the cheek of Jesus and places his evil mark on the Savior of the world. Before the soldiers' fists or the flogger's whips could leave their brutal scars, Judas left his.

The Lord could have made it to Calvary without the Judas detour. It would have been easy for the Roman soldiers to devise a way to capture the Nazarene without the betrayer's guided tour.

Originally, Jesus allowed Judas near when he called him as a disciple, and kept him close to his side for three significant years of earthly ministry. But, why would Jesus have allowed this deceitful person in his life?

For our sakes. By experiencing the agony of betrayal, Jesus incorporated our pain as his own. Each time a parent walks out the door, never to return for a goodnight kiss, Jesus understands that child's devastation. When a mate makes a mockery of the wedding vows, the Lord knows intimately the raw wound left behind. Tragically, when our best friend turns villain, Christ completely relates to that gut-wrenching stab.

Before he stumbled down the Via Dolorosa, the Lord was lacerated by a treacherous intent to harm. When you conclude that no one could possibly understand your desperate ache, think again. The Savior's blood was spilt after his perfect heart was broken in two.

ON THE RUN

"Therefore, if anyone cleanses himself from what
is dishonorable, he will be a vessel for honorable
use, set apart as holy, useful to the master of
the house, ready for every good work."
(2 Timothy 2:21)

Final words reverberate with enormous significance; sounds uttered as the body surrenders carry the weight of a lifetime. In the way Elijah's spirit spilled onto the shoulders of Elisha, the legacy of one man's parting words extends way beyond his own years. The apostle Paul, imprisoned in a Roman jail awaiting execution, showed us how to do this with the excellence that characterized his earthly existence.

Since his wrinkled hands could not extend beyond the prison doors, he used written words to impart his patriarchal blessing onto the head of his "beloved child." Paul penned his final letter to his spiritual son, Timothy, and gave him nourishment that we draw sustenance from today. The challenge laid out in the middle of the book beckons us to be "vessels of honor" as opposed to dishonorable ones. What would be some of the distinguishing marks of a life that is "useful to the master" and "ready for very good work?" What are the intricate details in our daily walk that will set us apart?

Paul teaches us to be cleansed of the contamination and contagiousness of sin, to "flee" from evil like a fugitive continually on the run. He compels us to be genuinely and unreservedly willing to be of service to the Master of the house. The apostle reminds us that humility, meekness, and compassion are the hallmarks of one who resembles the Savior from the inside out.

Whether we carry the elegant refinement of a sterling silver teapot or the sturdy, practical appeal of a brown plastic mixing bowl is irrelevant. Through Paul's final words, the Lord reminds us that he honors our wholehearted service as vessels that bear his name. He fills us with the power of his Spirit, pours himself through us, and uses us in small and grand ways because he "saved us and called us to a holy calling, not because of our works but because of his own purpose and grace, which he gave us in Christ Jesus before the ages began" (2 Timothy 1:9).

Words that are worth living by no matter our shape or size.

RESCUE OPERATION

"He who calls you is faithful; he will surely do it."
(I Thessalonians 5:24)

Halfway through the gospel of Matthew, one of Jesus' steady companions is starkly contrasted with an obscure woman. While the Gentile mother's faith towers over the long-standing disciple, God's hand powerfully rescued both from their dilemma.

Jesus is praying alone; the disciples are battling a raging storm. They are terrified when he approaches them, walking on the water, coming to their rescue. Peter asks permission to walk on the waves, too, and Jesus tells him, "Come." Yet, rather than continuing his gaze directly on the Master, Peter changes his focus to the ferocious winds and slides downward (Matthew 14:22-30).

Instantly, the passage tells us, Jesus grabs Peter, saving him from certain death. As Jesus is rescuing Peter, he admonishes him, "O you of little faith, why did you doubt?" Instantly, the winds cease their commotion the moment Christ enters the boat.

One chapter later, Christ praises the Syrophoenician woman for persistent faith. This mother begs Jesus to heal her demon-possessed daughter even as the disciples scorn her intrusion and demand her departure. She is relentless, and ignoring their disdain she insists on a miracle.

When Jesus explains that his primary responsibility is to the lost sheep of Israel, she kneels before him and humbly refers to herself as one unworthy of his intervention but needy nevertheless. She surprises Christ with her unwavering appeal, and he declares, "O woman, great is your faith. Be it done for you as you desire" (Matthew 15:28). Instantly, the Scriptures tell us, her daughter is healed.

In the middle of the storm Peter wavers, plummets, and is scolded by the Lord. In the midst of a young girl's demonic oppression, Christ salutes the Gentile mother who adamantly believes him for the impossible. Their faith varied, but God did not. Fear-filled Peter and the fearless woman both appealed to Jesus. He fixed his eyes on them and transformed their circumstances entirely by his power.

He still rescues; he still saves. Turbulent forces must still bow to his dominant authority.

PURSUIT

*"Therefore, as you received Christ Jesus the Lord, so walk
in him, rooted and built up in him and established in the
faith, just as you were taught, abounding in thanksgiving."*
(Colossians 2:6-7)

Clear directions give us a running head start. The patient teacher in kindergarten who painstakingly showed me how to print the first letter of my name, the basketball coach who drilled our daughter in the basics of dribbling down the court, and the driver's ed instructor who courageously careened down the highway by our son's side...each one doled out important directives to ensure we progressed successfully.

Saint Paul follows suit. In his letter to the Colossians, the apostle hands out a succinct list of what should occupy us after we have made certain that Christ Jesus is Lord of our lives.

First, keep walking in step with the Savior and live a lifestyle patterned after his. Walk like Jesus would; he left countless examples for us to imitate. Pick one, pursue it, and pursue it a bit more.

Then, draw nourishment from his life. Christ calls himself Living Water, the Bread of Life, and Honey from the rock; his Word is perfectly described as "pure spiritual milk." We are to crave the sustenance that he alone provides, to saturate ourselves with him in order to find full and complete satisfaction.

Paul finishes off his short list with a riveting phrase: "abounding in thanksgiving." Sometimes we neglect this key command, indifferent to its liberating force. As I develop a lifestyle of thankfulness, I combat greedy, materialistic urges.

With contentment as a framework, I will be less likely to gripe or complain, to whine or sulk over my petty circumstances.

In similar fashion, if I allow a spirit of gratefulness to permeate my relationships, my critical spirit will be short-circuited. When I applaud the beautiful etchings my friends have left on my life, I will be far less critical of their shortcomings.

Good teachers leave an indelible mark; we carry the words of the great ones with us for quite some time. But, when we strive to imitate the Master Teacher's words, our lives will honor the instructions summed up in his powerful phrase: "Follow me."

PART IV

YIELDING TO HIS WAY

"In all your ways acknowledge him, and he will make straight your paths."
Proverbs 3:6

SAND STORM

*"Some trust in chariots and some in horses, but
we trust in the name of the LORD our God."*
(Psalm 20:7)

Lions crouching at the door with tigers at your back…swarms of locusts overhead and quicksand beneath your feet are pictures of elusive escape routes without a rescuer in sight. The only sound slips between cracked lips as a faint whisper: "Help. Help me, Lord."

Long prayers have never been the prerequisite for Almighty God to move. His hand extends and clamps the lion's jaw. A fire blazes, and frightened tigers freeze.

He exhales a boisterous wind that blows locusts far off. And with his righteous right hand he grips your trembling frame; your location is unchanged, but now your companion is shield and bulwark.

Simply put, he is Savior. Strip away metaphors and dramatic scenes, and he remains steady, uncompromising, true. David knew of lions and bears. Their paws were practice for the enormous javelins and spears Goliath would one day wield.

The giant did not evaporate; the sling did not morph into a tank. But, the Spirit of the Living God empowered a faith-filled boy to accomplish the mighty feat of toppling the big man.

Later, the boy would be king. We still breathe his recorded prayers back to Almighty God. "May the Lord answer you in the day of trouble. May the name of the God of Jacob protect you! May he send you help from the sanctuary...May he grant you your heart's desire and fulfill all your plans" (Psalm 20:1-4). The giant held weapons in his hands. God held the boy in his. The latter trumps the former every time.

CRASHING THROUGH

"Open my eyes, that I may behold
wondrous things out of your law."
(Psalm 119:18)

S ome days, I approach the Scriptures simply as an act of obedience. With pen and journal on standby, I wait for inspiration
to fall from heaven and escort me to a spiritual retreat within
the confines of my comfortable family room. After a while I arise,
clutching only the satisfaction of showing up, not of being spiritually
satisfied.

On other days, the verses meander through my mind like sparkling water slipping over river rock, smoothing, caressing, cleansing
as they go. I am immersed in vibrant refreshment, drinking gulps to
ease a thirst that has no other remedy.

On other occasions words catapult off the sacred pages, landing
squarely before my eyes with the intensity of a lightning bolt. Familiar
words that have previously drifted by like invisible wisps of air now
take the form of a hurricane's wind force.

God's message blows into my heart with intensity, crashing
through the mediocre and the mundane, transforming my spirit by
its life-changing impact. Now, tucked into the lining of my mind are

portions of Scripture that are indelibly transcribed, that will nourish me continually, allowing me to extend to others this healing balm.

Sometimes I wait for God to show up in brilliant colors and splash vibrant hues across the canvas with a palette of jeweled-toned treasures. Often, black words on white onionskin pages are the only colors I see.

The drab and the dramatic have one thing in common: both occur when I choose to crack the cover and read.

PRECARIOUS

*"He is the radiance of the glory of God and the
exact imprint of his nature, and he upholds
the universe by the word of his power."
(Hebrews 1:3)*

The white envelope sat menacingly on my desk, daring me to read its contents. I eyed the suspicious return label for days, knowing perfectly well that a bureaucratic fine awaited me. Finally, I scanned the letter, acknowledged the impending consequence, and, with a heavy heart, called the department responsible.

After I explained my precarious position, I asked if anything could be done to rectify the situation. Was there a way to fix this problem? Could he explain what I should do next?

The calm voice on the other end assured me that he understood my predicament perfectly. Then he spoke six simple words: "I will take care of that." Incredulously, I rephrased my pressing need, certain that somehow I had been misunderstood. With a tone and manner that gave me confidence he had the authority to completely handle my case, he said again, "I will take care of that."

A hundred-pound boulder rolled off my chest; suddenly, everything around me seemed brighter, easier to manage. I cheerfully began to file the documents away but suddenly stopped with my hand beside the desk drawer.

Wasn't this precisely how my Father in Heaven would respond when I'd come barging into his presence with concerns that overwhelm me, with bewildering details that confound or confuse me? When I hoist my heavy loads onto his lap, when I cast my cares in his direction, invariably he, too, responds, "I will take care of that."

He reminds me throughout Scripture, "Call to me and I will answer you, and will tell you great and hidden things that you have not known" (Jeremiah 33:3)."Before they call I will answer; while they are yet speaking I will hear" (Isaiah 65:24). "But I call to God, and the LORD will save me. Evening, morning and noon I utter my complaint and moan, and he hears my voice" (Psalm 55:16-17).

Crystal clear and compelling, our Lord is perfectly able to handle questions, queries, and cumbersome loads, regardless of their height, depth, or heavy weight.

REFOCUS AND REALIGN

"Your way, O God, is holy. What God is great like
our God? You are the God who works wonders;"
(Psalm 77:13-14)

On most days, we pursue a frantic treadmill pace, with constant tumultuous noise buzzing in our ears from diverse, compelling sources. Distracted by this hectic combination, it proves difficult to focus on who is in charge and calling the shots.

Yet, if for a moment in the darkened stillness we crane our eyes toward the night sky, or gaze with slackened jaw at the unceasing slapping of wave water against rocky beach front, we may recall the Creator who works wonders without an ounce of our contribution. Considering the awe-inspiring grandeur of his sovereign rule is the antidote for anxious thoughts on multiple levels.

The Psalmist straightens out our crooked thoughts and realigns our confusion: "For who in the skies can be compared to the Lord? Who among the heavenly beings is like the Lord, a God greatly to be feared in the council of the holy ones, and awesome above all who are around him? O Lord God of hosts, who is mighty as you are, O Lord, with your faithfulness all around you?" (Psalm 89:6-8)

Our God is Sovereign King, and we bow to his majestic control over every last detail of his realm. As his beloved subjects, we recognize his authority and rest in the assurance that our High King reigns supreme, completely capable of managing our affairs along with the rest of the universe that he balances in his hands. "Cease striving and know that I am God," (Psalm 46:10) he reminds us over and over again, as we maneuver through the kingdom of Earth, with the Kingdom of Heaven in full view.

FAULT LINES

"Then Samson called to the LORD and said,
'O Lord GOD, please remember me and please
strengthen me only this once, O God...."
(Judges 16:28)

S amson is undoubtedly one of the more unsavory characters of the Old Testament, with little to recommend him in the way of discretion and sound judgment. It seems every glimpse of him reveals a portrait in selfishness and foolishness mixed in with a great deal of the ridiculous.

Perhaps the Lord throws in Samson's story to teach us what not to do, how not to waste his God-given gifts, handed out for his grand purpose and honor.

Endowed with superhuman strength, Samson was reared to deliver the Israelites from the jaws of their fierce enemies, the Philistines. With colossal courage and his bare hands, he tore lions apart, uprooted the gates of cities as if they were mere toothpicks, and annihilated 1,000 men with only a donkey's jawbone as weaponry.

He held limitless potential for good in the middle of his powerful hands, but he was powerless when it came to his own appetite and desires. In the end, intoxicated by the ways of women, Samson's very eyes were gouged out and his long curls shaved in his pursuit of all manner of evil. He squandered his golden opportunities, misguided by poor choices and plain, old-fashioned folly.

Remarkably, his name is listed in the chapter of faith in the very same sentence that extols heroes like Gideon, David, and Samuel (Hebrews 11:32) How could someone who consistently strayed from God's commandments, who blundered through life knocking over everyone in his path and ignoring God's directions, be placed in the paragraph that praises the faithfulness of Abraham and Moses?

Samson's shortcomings did not hamper God's will. In spite of those deficiencies, God's plan prevailed, and the enemies of the Israelites were confounded. Samson's mediocre life teaches us the ultimate consequences of unwise choices and simultaneously points to our Sovereign God, who uses donkeys to speak his Word and frail humans to accomplish his divine purposes.

This might give us hope as we maneuver through life and make our way, mistakes in hand, regrets in mind, and fault lines scattered around us.

SLIP AWAY

*"Now when Mary came to where Jesus was
and saw him, she fell at his feet...."*
(John 11:32)

Jesus is four days late, and his friends Martha and Mary are not exactly pleased.

Knowing their desperate need, he has not bothered to respond. It seems that Jesus is totally indifferent to their predicament and has left them out in the cold, in that dreadful place of disappointment.

In John chapter 11, we learn that their brother Lazarus is deathly ill; Jesus is notified about the dilemma, and he delays coming to their rescue intentionally.

When he finally makes an appearance, Martha sprints out of the house toward him with words that smack of accusation: "Lord, if you had been here, my brother would not have died" (John 11:21).

A few moments later, Martha notifies Mary that Jesus is calling. She, too, hurries to meet him, complaining with the exact words Martha used earlier. Behind their identical criticism, we can surmise their agonizing heartache as they nursed their brother, watched him slip away, prepared him for burial, and laid his lifeless body in a tomb.

Far more significantly than the similarity of their words is the way they respond to Jesus. In both scenes the women rush toward the

Lord, charge directly toward the only One who can make a difference. They are grievously disappointed with their outcome, aching from their loss, broken over their unanswered pleas. Yet they teach us precisely how to react when we are faced with stressful situations.

When nothing makes sense, when life is unfair, and when everything seems out of control, Mary and Martha exemplify how to respond. We, too, should run toward the Lord, throw ourselves on his mercy, and voice our complaint specifically in his direction.

Neither of the women ran away from the Lord. Nor did they keep silent. They did not remain where they were once they heard he was near. And when Jesus got ready to unlock the doorway to death, these two honest women were in the perfect position to witness the marvelous miracle he had intended all along.

DIVINE DIRECTIONS

"When the young man heard this he went away
sorrowful, for he had great possessions."
(Matthew 19:22)

Some Scriptures sag beneath the weight of regret-filled words. Encumbered with misgivings, a scent of deep sadness seeps through the verses like a vine overloaded with fruit too burdensome to bear.

In one unforgettable scene, we meet a young man as he approaches Christ with the question, "Teacher, what good deed must I do to have eternal life?" (Matthew 19:16) No wiser question has ever been asked, no wiser counsel ever sought.

Face to face with the Son of God, one on one with the Master Teacher, the young man's self-importance prevents him from accepting divine directions. Jesus lays out an exact prescription for his malady, explaining all he needs to know to follow him and find life eternal.

The man's response to Christ is pitiful indeed. "When the young man heard this, he went away sorrowful, for he had great possessions." We want to beckon to him, prevent him from making this tragic mistake. We long to say, "Turn back. The King himself is giving you the keys to unlock the doorway to heaven." But, we are incapable of rescuing this young man. Even Christ the Messiah let him walk away, never forcing him to accept his perfect plan. The lessons learned make us mindful of the questioning ones who travel our way. We are called to direct them to Jesus as the source of life eternal, to share his Word and the great plan revealed for all.

At the same time, we are reminded to leave the outcome to Him.

LIMPING ALONG

"Now the Word of the LORD came to Jonah the son of Amittai, saying, 'Arise, go to Nineveh, that great city, and call out against it, for their evil has come up before me.' But Jonah rose to flee to Tarshish from the presence of the LORD."
(Jonah 1:1-3)

We instantly recognize the familiar, fishy story of Jonah. God asked this reluctant messenger to go, but he ran away instead, where the storm blew wild, and the fish gulped him whole. Whereas all God's other creations of sea, fish, and worm were willing to obey his precise bidding, Jonah only halfheartedly obliged.

The prophet's shrimp-like faith limped along, in direct contrast to the narrative's mega-sized participants: the ferocious storm, the enormous fish, the prosperous city, and the 120,000 repentant inhabitants. That's before we even contemplate God's extravagant capacity to forgive.

The final chapter opens with these compelling words: "But it displeased Jonah exceedingly, and he was angry." He loathed the ruthless Ninevites and despised Jehovah for saving their measly lives. How dare God redeem such undeserving enemies! Why had Jonah bothered to come, if Jehovah would rescue them regardless? The nerve of God, to do what Jonah thought unfair; he figured God could not be trusted.

Seen in this light, Jonah appears silly and childish. He disapproved of God's actions and was grievously disappointed by the circumstances God orchestrated. Yet are we any different? Each time we balk at God's unwelcome decisions, we imitate the immature prophet.

Isn't our heart as foul as Jonah's when we are faced with unpleasant scenarios? When God veers from our instructions and expectations, we find it more conducive to treat him with contempt than to embrace his will and his ways. If we are honest, we will recognize Jonah-pride as it thrashes its ugly tail. But, if we refrain from complaining, we will recognize that we cannot force God's hand to do our bidding.

Recall the challenge in Isaiah 55:8-9: "'For my thoughts are not your thoughts, neither are your ways my ways,' declares the Lord. 'As the heavens are higher than the earth, so are my ways higher than your ways and my thoughts than your thoughts.'"

God probes Jonah and our hearts, too, when He asks, "Do you do well to be angry?" That's a question we would be wise to consider and answer as well.

MARCHING ORDERS

*"You did not choose me, but I chose you and
appointed you that you should go and bear
fruit and that your fruit should abide...."*
(John 15:16)

We long to hear God's voice, to understand what he wants us to be about, to figure out his will and his ways for our life. We complicate the matter most of the time by looking for signs, questioning our own motives, and doubting his plan.

The Lord's clear voice slices through the confusion like a sharpened steel sword, leaving little room for reservations. Uncertainty dissipates, and we are left marked with a charge as forthright and convincing as if he actually handed us written marching orders. In black and white, we read his powerful call: "You did not choose me, but I chose you and appointed you that you should go and bear fruit, and that your fruit should remain." The Lord clarifies our relationship: he selected us for a special mission, a purpose only we can fulfill. He chose us by appointment for the specific task of bearing fruit, for accomplishing what is eternally significant.

What is this fruit he desires? What can we invest our lives in that will outlast us and soar into eternity? People: loving them, leading them, guiding them to the Savior...touching them with the remarkable, life-changing power of the Gospel and helping them to recognize other pursuits as far less worthy. Plowing this soil is hard work; weeding, fertilizing, and watering all take time. Pruning, shaping, and trimming are essential for a healthy harvest.

The payoff is the fruit…bushels of men and women walking with the Savior who are eager to do his will and who understand that he has chosen them for such a time as this.

Father, make us aware of the men and women you bring across our path. Guide our efforts so we make worthwhile investments in their lives. Pour your Spirit through us and make our lives an orchard laden with your fruit of righteousness. Keep us from discouragement when the work is hard. Remind us that you are in charge. May our lives be marked by obedience, regardless.

WOODEN STAKES

*"God, the Lord, is my strength; he makes my feet like
the deer's; he makes me tread on my high places."*
(Habakkuk 3:19)

I ran headlong into old friends this week – caught sight of them
when I wasn't even looking or aware of how much I needed their
familiar faces. Knowing what they held, they came searching for
me.

In the way photographs stir forgotten memories and reopen the
past for current viewing, these two friends unlocked a door; over the
threshold they strode, settled themselves before me, and visited as if
no time had elapsed since they last kept me company.

I was seventeen when I first noticed them, green in my faith, uncertain of the future. I began falling in love with the Lord then and
he, pursuing me with passion, opened my sights to the wonder of his
words.

I kept a journal, a simple notebook where I penned meaningful
portions of Scripture, the ones that held my gaze and stirred noble
aspirations within my youthful heart. Here I scrawled significant verses that marked me like wooden stakes the Lord hammered inside me.

In the obscure pages where my fingers still fumble, I read once
more: "Though the fig tree should not blossom, nor fruit be on the

vines, the produce of the olive fail and the fields yield no food, the flock be cut off from the fold and there be no herd in the stalls, yet I will rejoice in the LORD; I will take joy in the God of my salvation… he makes my feet like the deer's; he makes me tread on high places" (Habakkuk 3:17-19).

Thirty-five years later, I am transported to my teenage bedroom and the beginning stage of my spiritual journey. Clueless of what was ahead I understood then that regardless of barren fields and infertile years, despite hardships and hard ways, I need not fear. The God who had saved me would always be Savior; the God who had rescued me would always be Rescuer and Friend.

This week, I looked steadily again at these unchanging truths and celebrated their unwavering reality — every word accurate, their meaning proven and tried.

Especially in the unfruitful, unyielding, blossom-barren times, the Lord was provider and friend. Every promise he nailed down, he enforced. He brought joy when circumstances dictated otherwise and gave relief amidst disarray.

He had given me his Word and kept it, taken my hand and held it. I must choose to trust him still, for the journey on from here.

AIM TO PLEASE

"And he died for all, that those who live might
no longer live for themselves, but for him who
for their sake died and was raised."
(2 Corinthians 5:15)

Sometimes, seated on soft cushioned seats in air-conditioned sanctuaries, it is easy to suppose that others are essential to God's purposes but our contributions are unnecessary or irrelevant. Nothing could be further from the truth.

On mission trips in foreign lands, where peculiar and out-of-the-ordinary is commonplace, each person is keenly aware that he or she is paramount to the success of the endeavor. But, in comfortable surroundings where life is jammed with routine responsibilities, our passionate pursuits can be tamed by the ordinary.

The men who blazed Christianity from the outside of the empty tomb to the far reaches of the Roman world were never accused of being mediocre or tame.

They recognized the urgency in being believers God could entrust with the message of reconciliation, through whom he could make his appeal. They continue to call to us through the pages of history and the Words of Scripture. "We make it our aim to please him. For we must all appear before the judgment seat of Christ…knowing the fear of the Lord, we persuade others" (2 Corinthians 5:9-11).

Living for ourselves is easy. Nothing to it, really! However, the adventure of a lifetime belongs to those willing to risk obeying his voice through the clamor, those striving to reach places others only glimpse far, far ahead.

COSTLY WALK

"Do not be slothful in zeal, be fervent
in spirit, serve the Lord."
(Romans 12:11)

God longs for us to know him intimately and make him known to others. Throughout the Gospels, Christ challenges us to accomplish this by a life of faithful "following" after him. In order to give us a clear visual of what this type of obedience looks like, he inspired Luke to record details of the apostle Paul's ministry in the book of Acts. Clearly Paul was a man who recognized that unwavering perseverance was essential for God's mandate to be fulfilled.

While Paul was in Corinth, "he reasoned in the synagogue every Sabbath, and tried to persuade Jews and Greeks" (Acts 18:4). He didn't wave a magic wand and effortlessly manufacture an assortment of converts to his side. Obedience to the Father's will required persistence and demanded sacrifice.

Saint Paul was eloquent, intelligent, and educated. Jesus called him to a daring assignment through a blinding light on the road to Damascus. Still, Paul had to keep showing up in the synagogue week after week, "trying to persuade" those who were not too thrilled with his message.

Sharing the Gospel took an enormous amount of time, energy, and effort for the apostle, with no guarantee of success. Why, then, are we so easily discouraged when our efforts appear to produce dismal returns? The faithful Christian walk requires a costly investment, and God alone tallies the victories.

Paul's perseverance reminds us that we must continue doing the Father's work, even when the results do not appear, from our limited perspective, to be favorable.

INTERTWINED

*"And because he was of the same trade he stayed with
them and worked, for they were tentmakers by trade."*
(Acts 18:3)

Usually, when we need a spark of encouragement, a scriptural vitamin-B shot to extinguish our physical or spiritual malaise, we plunge into the poetry of the Psalms. Surprisingly, and where we least expect it, God often uses a seemingly mundane portion of Scripture to bolster our courage.

Tucked into the fabric of Acts 18 is a principle that can strengthen our resolve. The chapter focuses on Paul's obedience, his life of surrender to the cause of Christ, and his unflinching abandonment to the Father's will. Intertwined in this passage is a succinct job description of a disciple of Christ. In verse 3, Luke notes that Paul was a tentmaker by trade. The famous apostle did not hold the office of an important politician or prestigious professional. He wasn't part of the religious elite or the wealthy aristocrats but was simply a craftsman.

God's bold witness for the Gospel, who radically affected the world for Christ's sake, made ends meet by stitching tents. Looking at Paul, we learn that God's requirement for faithful service is not an impressive career or exalted occupation. The tentmaker teaches us to pursue obedience and a surrendered will.

As we maneuver through our regular routines, fulfilling God's agenda, Paul's life is a reminder that ordinary is okay.

TO THAT END

*"Hear, my son, your father's instruction, and forsake
not your mother's teaching, for they are a graceful
garland for your head and pendants for your neck."*
(Proverbs 1:8-9)

My father took the book of Proverbs seriously, and it marked his character like falling rain drenches a well-tilled field. Yanked from school at an early age, he was forbidden to continue because of his deteriorating eyesight. "Teach him a trade," the doctor advised, squelching forever my father's dream of becoming a physician.

King Solomon's volume became his rulebook and mentor. The verses counseled him, guarded his steps, directed him where to go and precisely how to get there. "Keep your heart with all vigilance, for from it flow the springs of life…Ponder the path of your feet, then all your ways will be sure. Do not swerve to the right or the left; turn your foot away from evil" (Proverbs 4:23, 26-27). He inhaled the wisdom of the words and lined up his life accordingly.

I watched him from within the confines of our home, saw him deal fairly with his staff and generously with many others. The garments of industry and endurance draped his shoulders, and he discreetly opened his wallet to those who he discovered were in need.

In his final days cancer withered his frame, but loving hands meticulously cared for him. All of his children and twenty grandchildren stood attentively by his side. And when his assignment on earth was through, my father slipped away from us peacefully, his mind and heart bright and clear to the end. "Whoever brings blessing will be enriched, and one who waters will himself be watered" (Proverbs 11:25).

The Word of God fulfilled throughout his life and all the way through, to death.

PARCEL OF LAND

"And David built there an altar to the LORD
and offered burnt offerings and peace offerings.
So the LORD responded to the plea...."
(2 Samuel 24:25)

King David's unparalleled intimacy with Almighty God did not prevent him from making drastic mistakes. In fact, the tumultuous ups and downs that mark the life of the shepherd king might prompt us to wonder why God labeled him "a man after my own heart, who will do all my will" (Acts 13:22).

We admire him as insightful poet, courageous warrior, and loyal friend, but we are dismayed at his adulterous affair with Bathsheba and heinous murder of her husband Uriah. His chronically neglectful parenting, with its disastrous fallout, leaves us bewildered as well.

Yet, when David recognizes his own wrongdoing, his true character emerges, and we witness his contrite heart pleading for forgiveness. When Nathan the prophet confronts him after his royal downfall with Bathsheba, our own hearts concur as David agrees with God, "Against you, you only, have I sinned and done what is evil in your sight, so that you may be justified in your words and blameless in your judgment" (Psalm 51:4).

Years afterward, against God's direct orders, conceited David demands a census of his warriors. Nine months and twenty days later, his army commander Joab hands him the results: Israel and Judah have a combined 1,300,000 warriors.

David immediately cries out, " I have sinned greatly in what I have done. But now, O LORD, please take away the iniquity of your servant, for I have done foolishly" (2 Samuel 24:10).

The consequence for this disobedience is the death of 70,000 men from Dan to Beersheba. To avert further calamity, David attempts to purchase the designated threshing floor from Araunah in order to build an altar. The owner gladly promises to give him the parcel of land and everything else necessary for the sacrifice at no cost, but David declines the gracious offer.

"No, but I will buy it from you for a price," David responds. "I will not offer burnt offerings to the LORD my God that cost me nothing."

David's compelling words raise a standard for us to follow. His recorded prayers expose us to true repentance: "Create in me a clean heart, O God, and renew a right spirit within me...Restore to me the joy of your salvation and uphold me with a willing spirit" (Psalm 51:10-12).

O God, we need you to create clean hearts, right spirits, right ways in each of us as well. We beg for your mercy to renew and restore all our patched and broken places. Bring David's repentant cry to our minds when we stray from you. Let us offer to you what costs us something. You gave us what cost you everything.

FRAIL FOLLOWERS

"In the same way, let your light shine before
others, so that they may see your good works and
give glory to your Father who is in heaven."
(Matthew 5:16)

Jesus Christ called his followers to act like him. He embodied sacrificial love, uncompromising truth, and tender compassion among many other remarkable traits. I saw him clearly this week, caught some of his followers demonstrating that they were image-bearers of the incomparable Savior. Seeing his reflection in their lives made me long to slip off shoes as I realized I was standing on holy ground in the most ordinary of places.

The news filtered through that my aunt's hours on earth were dwindling fast; each labored breath was like the final grains of sand rushing through the hourglass at a maddening pace. She was barely a wisp beneath crumpled sheets, her life almost completely spent. Two daughters stood at the bedside on full alert, their hands aching to ease her pain, their presence caressing her through the midnight stretch of darkness. Had she not held them so when they were cherished infants? Once she had attended their every need; now, it was their pleasure to return the favor.

The widow stood beneath a halo of light, a small, white-haired warrior in the fight to slay complacency and indifference to the Word. At times, the heavy weight of responsibility to convey the meaning within the sacred pages crushes her. She labors under the strain of the battle, unswerving determination matched by unfaltering devotion for the Master who equips her for the task. The twinkling light in her aged eyes and her insightful lessons both convey that she is an "instrument of righteousness" in the Savior's hands.

The single businesswoman has never worn a wedding ring or borne a child of her own. Yet, whenever the church's nursery doors open for services or Bible studies, she carefully tends the little ones as if they carried her name. Tireless and capable, she soothes, rocks, and feeds. She drops to her knees beside the toddlers, swaddles the babies close, and somehow has the magical touch that makes wailing children trust her with a toothy smile. Few applaud her efforts now; fewer still realize the cost of her faithful service. Still that will not keep her from fulfilling the high calling to the Lord, who declared, "Let the children come to me, and do not hinder them...." (Matthew 19:14)

Lord of all goodness, fill us with the brilliance of your love. In spite of our shortcomings, pour yourself through our simple efforts. May your face be seen and your voice heard as we strive to follow you in service and sacrifice and love.

FAMILIAR PASSAGE

"Therefore, we are ambassadors for Christ,
God making his appeal through us."
(2 Corinthians 5:20)

W hen God's children cluster around open Bibles with their handwritten notes strewn across circular tables, a distinct beauty emerges. Laughter filters from one group; robust discussion erupts from another. Side by side, they discover surprising details from a familiar passage or contemplate the significance of a principal that, if applied, could radically affect their worlds.

The fragrance of concerns unveiled in prayer rises from their midst. They lift one another to the only One capable of healing, helping, and making all things new. On behalf of family members they might never meet, they intercede as an act of obedience to the God who rules the universe and calms turbulent storms. Their pleas ascend like poured-out perfume, and they watch for God to orchestrate his sovereign plan.

Fruit tastes sweet, the fruit of the Spirit sweeter yet. As followers of Christ look out for the hurting, they encircle one another with acts of compassion. Kindness listens and eases the crushing weight, the paralyzing confusion. The touch of gentleness remains long after one hand extends nourishment to another.

Working together, hauling the load in unison, serving as a team, men and women demonstrate the sacrificial spirit of corporate service. Let me help you with that, and together we can carry it farther down the road. I will lift the bundle you are buckling beneath to keep you from being overwhelmed.

Are you committed to a cause to demonstrate Christ's love to a desperate world? Show me how I can assist. Two can maneuver faster than one. Ten can manage further still. Together, let us touch the world around us for the sake of the Gospel.

Do you hear that sound? It is the voices of angels celebrating. The believers are serving each other as they serve their Lord, and suddenly, in small and grand ways, others are taking notice. Drawn in, intrigued by what they sense, others will long to know the Savior. Listen closely as I tell you what he has done for me; allow me to share what I am learning through his Word. Are you curious that I have joy despite the mundane? Let me direct you to the source. Jesus is calling your name and longs for you to respond to his voice.

When the gospel is proclaimed with the beauty of obedience, the strength of compassion, and the measure of sacrifice, followers of Christ fulfill their purpose and revolutionize their world, one life at a time.

ROCKY GROUND

"And he said, 'He who has ears to hear, let him hear.'"
(Mark 4:9)

C hrist understood his audience would grasp a good story quicker than a lengthy lecture and used illustrations listeners could easily identify. Perhaps as he lifted his eyes above the gathered throng and saw the farmland, he drew inspiration for this parable. He spoke of ordinary soils and seeds, and yet the meaning eluded the assembled crowds. Even the disciples missed the point and went to him afterward for further clarification.

"Do you not understand this parable? How then will you understand all the parables?" (Mark 4:13) His words probe our hearts as well. *Where are your spiritual ears which are essential to comprehend spiritual truth? Where are your spiritual eyes to see through the obvious, to dive beneath the surface and unearth the true meaning lingering beneath?*

Do not take my words lightly. What sort of field lies within your heart? Are you an indifferent path, where the seed of the Word cannot take root because no soil lies there? Is your heart so shallow, covered with the faintest layer of soil, that you quickly grab the message and just as quickly abandon it? Are you thorn-infested, controlled by all culture has to offer, allowing my words to wither within the briar patch of your pursuits of wealth and importance?

Allow me to plant my words deep into your prepared heart, broken up by life's disappointments, tilled by struggle and heartache, furrowed by trials and tests. Such soil will yield a crop thirty, sixty, or a hundred times over.

In response, we pray: "Father, we beg you to sow your message in the soil of our souls. In your divine way, bury seed and cause us to sprout a harvest. Make our hearts pliable, teachable, accepting of what you place within. Protect us from becoming irrelevant paths or from turning into rocky, hard ground. May you never have opportunity to say our lives "yielded no grain."

That's a landscape we never want as part of our story.

GOD'S WAY

""A good name is to be chosen rather than great riches, and favor is better than silver or gold…Do you see a man skillful in his work? He will stand before kings; he will not stand before obscure men."
(Proverbs 22:1,29)

Like electrifying lightning bolts etched across a midnight sky, the opening and closing statements of Proverbs 22 are charged with significance. Pursuing virtue and diligence are worthy goals. Interestingly, two of the most memorable characters in the Old Testament exemplified these qualities, standing fearlessly before royalty on behalf of the God they served.

Daniel and Joseph endured the horrific ordeal of being yanked from their homeland and forced to serve in a foreign setting far, far away from anything familiar or comfortable. But, like gold purified by immersion in flames, their lives illuminated their pagan surroundings.

The Bible tells us, "The LORD was with Joseph…his master saw that the LORD was with him and that the LORD caused all that he did to succeed in his hands" (Genesis 39:2-3). After only one conversation with Joseph and recognizing that the "Spirit of God" dwelt in him, Pharaoh handed over the reins of the entire Egyptian government to this former incarcerated slave.

Daniel's path ran parallel to Jacob's lost son. Each of the men possessed beauty, brains, and breeding, yet with a spirit of utmost humility honored the Lord in his actions and words. After Daniel first revealed and then interpreted the king's dream, Nebuchadnezzar, "fell upon his face and paid homage to Daniel." The king's next words were as extraordinary as his actions: "Truly, your God is God of gods and Lord of kings" (Daniel 2:47).

The men walked without a hint of compromise and brought honor to God's holy name. They worked skillfully on behalf of the Living God, representing him with integrity in the smallest details. Is it any wonder that their names and character shine brighter than ever after all these centuries?

Go ahead. Do it God's way. Ultimately, the King who matters will take notice, too.

WAIT AWHILE

*"A woman from Samaria came to draw water.
Jesus said to her, "Give me a drink."*
(John 4:7)

Christ handled people with brilliant insight. In this story of an ancient Eastern unbeliever, we hear his heart in our hectic Western world.

The Samaritan woman entered this familiar place without suspecting her life would be transformed. Perhaps because her reputation prevented her from mingling with the upright ladies of the village earlier in the day, she arrived at the odd time of noon. Before Christ confronted her with his life-altering message, he grabbed her attention with a request to quench his thirst.

She was the one truly parched; her choices had left her spiritually dehydrated. The source of Living Water beckoned to her with an appeal, all the while focused on giving her, "a spring of water welling up to eternal life" (John 4:14b). No record exists that she ever handed him a cup – there is no clue that she ever met his need but all the evidence in the world that he met hers.

With similar intent, he summons us today. "Will you wait awhile, adjust your routine, and give me a portion of your day? Will you allow me to satisfy your longings with what is pure and divine?"

Christ's essence is marked by extravagant generosity. He has no needs, but sometimes he requests something ordinary from us, like our time and our attention. We can still encounter him today, right where we are, pitcher in hand, reputation imperfect. Wait as he poses the questions; remember that his answers lead to life eternal in measureless ways.

SURRENDERED MARCH

"Then Pilate said to him, 'So you are a king?'
Jesus answered, 'You say that I am a king. For this
purpose I was born and for this purpose I have come
into the world – to bear witness to the truth.'"
(John 18:37)

Wise men hold the distinction of asking great questions. The magi were no exception. When they came seeking Jesus, they posed one of those perfectly intelligent questions that even today beg to be answered: "Where is he who has been born king of the Jews?" (Matthew 2:2)

Herod the fool sought counsel and directed the travelers to Bethlehem. But, in the unfolding events of the Gospel, the complete answer becomes apparent.

Where exactly is he who was born king of the Jews? The Scriptures' reply is plain enough.

There he is, in Galilee, "teaching in their synagogues and proclaiming the gospel of the kingdom and healing every disease and every affliction among the people" (Matthew 4:23). Watch for him as "great crowds follow him from Galilee and the Decapolis, and from Jerusalem and Judea, and from beyond the Jordan" (Matthew 4:25). See him in Capernaum as the Roman centurion appeals for healing for his paralyzed servant. Jesus' compassionate response exposes his true character.

Inundated with enormous responsibilities, pressurized by endless needs, the king of the Jews willingly responds, "I will come and heal him."

Read Matthew's account in chapters 14 and 15, and see his divine movements as he, "withdrew from there in a boat to a desolate place… and withdrew to the district of Tyre and Sidon…went on from there and walked beside the Sea of Galilee…." Jesus was fulfilling the Father's will far from the crowds, on his surrendered march toward Jerusalem.

Now, where is he who was born king of the Jews? At a place called Golgotha where they crucify him, divide up his garments, and nail the criminal charge directly over his head: "Jesus of Nazareth, the King of the Jews" (John 19:19). The very phrase the magi used thirty-some years earlier is written now in Aramaic, Latin, and Greek. No one need miss the message.

The answer to the probing question doesn't end at the cross, though. On the third day when the women come to his tomb, two dazzling angels explain, "Why do you seek the living among the dead? He is not here, but has risen" (Luke 24:5b-6). Breaking the barriers of sin and death, the King of the Jews has forever unlocked the answers to life eternal.

Ask yourself the wise men's question: where is the King of the Jews in your own life? Is he sidelined as irrelevant or inconvenient, or is he the central figure in your daily existence? Where you place him is really still a matter of life and death.

CAUTION

"You save a humble people, but your eyes are
on the haughty to bring them down."
(II Samuel 22:28)

The threads of humility embroidered in a person's character are like strands of silver, attracting far more attention than arrogance's peacock feathers ever could. We catch glimpses of this striking quality in Joseph as he forgives his brothers' treachery, in Daniel's uncompromising choices in a pagan land, and in Paul's concern for those who labor beside him as the early church first begins to soar.

Submission, obedience, and service all thrive when rooted in the soil of humility. Paul encourages wives to submit, husbands to love, fathers to caution, children to obey, and slaves to serve their masters willingly. He heightens the charge to each with encouragement to view these relationships in the glow that radiates from humility's perspective. "Whatever you do, work heartily as for the Lord and not for men, knowing that from the Lord you will receive the inheritance as your reward. You are serving the Lord Christ" (Colossians 3:23-24).

Paul does not simply dictate humility for others like a physician needlessly prescribing medication; he lives it. Chains bind him to a prison cell, and yet he demonstrates humility by his concern and appreciation for his fellow workers.

Rather than elevating himself, he gives honor to a dozen believers who work alongside him.

With tenderness, Paul refers to them as "beloved brothers," "fellow servants," and "faithful ministers." Tychicus, Onesimus, Aristarchus, and a long list of others crown the end of this letter like valuable jewels. All are essential to the cause of the Gospel, each one fulfilling the purpose God has set before them.

Oftentimes, we become discouraged with the call to service and submission. The daunting challenge may overwhelm us or seem outdated at best. But, in remembering that our first priority is to serve the Lord Jesus Christ in everything, the other commands fall into place. We belong to him. He is our true Master. Our loving service to others is simply a sincere and humble offering we present to him.

Lord of our hearts, would you infuse your humility through us so others looking on will catch a glimpse of you as we serve and submit and surrender.

COMMON FLOW

"His mother said to the servants, 'Do whatever he tells you.'"
(John 2:5)

Sometimes we wonder what obedience looks like, how it might sound, and how exactly to do it when it is easier said than done. A few lowly servants illustrate it precisely at that miraculous wedding in Cana of Galilee.

The feast is in full swing when the wine dissipates. Mary is concerned and brings the problem to Jesus. At first it seems that Christ will do nothing to fix the dilemma; he responds curiously, "Woman, what does this have to do with me? My hour has not yet come" (John 2:4). Yet, something in his tone, something in the expression that passed between them, convinced the mother that her son would act. She immediately instructs the servants, "Do whatever he tells you."

They obey. The servants jump into action and fill six stone water jars to the brim. They couldn't turn on a faucet to accomplish the feat but had to haul the 120 to 180 gallons from a well. That took time, effort, and energy. They didn't necessarily understand what would result but obeyed anyway.

Jesus never commanded the water to change into wine. He did not wave his hand over the jars to transform the ordinary into the extraordinary. His only commands were to the servants, to "fill up " and "draw out" and "take to."

The humble servants received the greatest wedding gift – not the bridegroom whose reputation was salvaged, nor the guests who were treated to the finest. The servants knew who had performed the miracle. They were eyewitnesses to the common water flowing into the containers and the delectable wine flowing out. They encountered Jesus by the jars, obeyed his voice, and would never be the same.

The next time the Lord asks something of you or reveals a new direction for you to follow, remember the wedding-day lesson. Just "do whatever he tells you."

SURROUNDING FOG

"While they were talking and discussing together,
Jesus himself drew near and went with them. But
their eyes were kept from recognizing him."
(Luke 24:15-16)

Often we resemble the two disciples on the road to Emmaus. Downcast, we trudge along, walking away from our own confusing Jerusalem, where things have not gone as we expected.

In the fog that surrounds our circumstances we may misunderstand exactly what God is allowing. Like those two favored ones, we fail to comprehend that he journeys beside us, waiting to reveal himself in his perfect time.

What is it that keeps us from recognizing him? Like that pair of ancient followers, we ask the Lord incredulously, "Do you not know the things that have happened in these days?"

As if he did not fully comprehend what had just taken place on the cross and in the tomb, they instructed him in what he already knew by heart. Ignorantly, they believed him to be uninformed and out of touch. Do we not treat him with similar disdain when we attempt to enlighten him about our complex lives?

He rebuked them, and he rightfully rebukes us, too. "O foolish ones, and slow of heart to believe..." (Luke 24:25) How illogical to act as if the Creator of the Universe is powerless to work on our behalf.

Like those two comrades of old, let us implore the Lord "to stay" and open the Scriptures to us so our hearts may burn. As we wait for him, he will reveal to us as well that he is in our midst, on the dusty road, in the middle of our journey, home.

CLODS AND DUST

"I bless the LORD who gives me counsel; in the night
also my heart instructs me. I have set the LORD
always before me; because he is at my right hand,
I shall not be shaken."
(Psalm 16:7-8)

Pebbles of wisdom matched against boulders of truth; a spattering of know- how confronting limitless understanding; little droplets of sense filtering by an overflowing ocean tide of what really matters – clearly, no comparison exists between man's finite mind and the grand source of perfect wisdom found in God.

Most of life's peevish complaints crumble like brittle clay when confronted by God's masterful perspective. With a poet's eloquence and a swordsman's precise thrust, the Lord exposes mankind's acute ignorance in his dialogue with Job. "Has the rain a father, or who has begotten the drops of dew? From whose womb did the ice come forth, and who has given birth to the frost of heaven?" (Job 38:28-29)

Relentless in his attack on the foolishness of doubting him, God lays before Job dozens of scenarios to illustrate his unparalleled magnificence. "Who can number the clouds by wisdom? Or who can tilt the water skins of the heavens, when the dust runs into a mass and the clods stick fast together? Is it by your understanding that the hawk soars and spreads his wings toward the south? Is it at your command that the eagle mounts up and makes his nest on high?" (Job 38:37-38; 39:26-27)

Job gets God's point perfectly and tutors us on how to respond when we doubt God's goodness or his management of our affairs: "I know that you can do all things, and that no purpose of yours can be thwarted...Therefore I have uttered what I did not understand, things too wonderful for me, which I did not know" (Job 42:2-3).

When our thinking needs realignment, when our thoughts beg direction, when what we lack is a good dose of God's viewpoint, let us remember Job's advise and line ourselves up with our God who is absolutely in charge of all the particulars we do "not understand."

MADDENING PACE

"Trust in him at all times, O people; pour out
your heart before him; God is a refuge for us."
(Psalm 62:8)

Our culture bombards us with the urgent noise of a relentless siren. News programs squawk the moment our eyes flicker open; traffic reports blare from the car radio; electronic devices drain life out of other meaningful moments. Every spot on the street and in our homes is wired for sound. We are fully entertained, galloping at a maddening rate and completely exhausted. What is the remedy? What innovative contraption can we invent next to relieve the clamor and the pace?

The answer is as timeless as the Creator himself. One unheeded verse in the Psalms provides the prescription: "For God alone, O my soul, wait in silence, for my hope is from him" (Psalm 62:5). King David uncovered the antidote to many of our 21st-century ailments. Three words sum it up: wait in silence. Be still and be quiet long enough to hear from Almighty God.

Our spirits are famished, our senses impoverished. We crave the very thing our Creator wired us for – alone time with him. Distracted by the ceaseless clamor on every side, we fail to give him the necessary time to nourish us. Preoccupied with our own chattering, we neglect the sacred call to be silent.

His voice beckons to us, "Come to me, all who labor and are heavy laden, and I will give you rest" (Matthew 11:28). The first step involves a conscious choice to approach Christ, recognizing that we cart around the cumbersome burden of confusion and wait quietly before him. He takes care of the second part...extending rest and stillness as a peaceful balm to the noise outside and within.

Lord of sacred silence, you are able to still my noisy world. Reign in the raucous all around and extend to me a quiet and a calm you alone are able to provide. Help me to put aside distractions and cease my frantic pace so you can remind me again of the wonders I can find with you.

MARCHING IN

"The eyes of the LORD are toward the
righteous and his ears toward their cry."
(Psalm 34:15)

O n Sunday mornings, the group gathers adjacent to the sanctuary. Ordinary folk trickle in, find a seat, and wait their turn. Empty hands folded on laps, they speak in hushed tones, armed for battle, brandishing their unseen weapons.

It is early morning in the prayer room. Before the service begins or the worship rolls out in exalted choruses of praise, a few huddle together with the sole purpose of marching into the throne room to access that limitless supply of grace.

We are children making requests of our benevolent Father, servants eager to please, pilgrims longing to know the route to follow, fishermen desiring the souls of men and women, sinners in desperate need of the Holy One's cleansing and forgiveness. Boldly we approach, dressed in a righteousness unearned and undeserved, washed in the blood-soaked covering of the Lamb, recognizing our complete inadequacy to meet one need, to make anything happen apart from the divine intervention of Almighty God. Like brothers and sisters pressing close to the Father, we bring our requests and lay them before the

Maker of Heaven and Earth. Children of the Living God, we "Taste and see that the LORD is good!" (Psalm 34:8)

At the last "amen," we filter through the crowded lobby and join those seated for worship. Our appearance is unchanged, but don't be fooled. Our hearts are tenderized, and our eyes have glimpsed the reality of the Kingdom of Heaven smack-dab in the midst of a regular Sunday morning.

ONGOING

"And the Lord will guide you continually and satisfy
your desire in scorched places and make your bones
strong; and you shall be like a watered garden, like
a spring of water, whose waters do not fail."
(Isaiah 58:11)

Every now and then, when I least expect it and have almost forgotten its poetic richness and refreshment, I stumble across Isaiah 58:11. With the pleasure of recognizing a long-lost, treasured friend, I reread the words and inhale deep satisfaction for spirit and soul.

"And the Lord will guide you continually...." Go ahead of us, dear Lord. Lead and guide as our capable, distinguished Guidance Counselor. Go ahead, take the lead. You take no breaks from your role... you are constant, unlimited, unchecked, and ongoing.

"And satisfy your desire in scorched places...." You bring satisfaction, a filling up to the brim, a river of gladness and fulfillment of desires that you have placed within. Your work is accomplished in the place where scarcely any hope remains, where life has been scorched, blistered, and perhaps even ruined. Where anxiety lurks, roller coasters collide, and endless expectations abound, you measure out contentment in gallon helpings.

"And make your bones strong...." You provide strength for the heavy task and the cumbersome load. You made Joseph strong to bear up beneath the agony of slavery and imprisonment. You gave Daniel the fortitude not to bend his knee to pagan gods. Esther stood up to her tyrant king, and Ruth gleaned in a foreign land.

You made their bones strong to endure, to persevere, and to accomplish your will regardless. You promise to do the same for us.

"And you shall be like a watered garden...." Lush and fragrant, a green and fruitful landscape, watered well by springs that bubble from beneath the earth.

As you guide, we are satisfied; where scorching heat should destroy, you strengthen and provide. All the while, you are transforming our lives into a garden of beauty, to nourish the souls of others who stroll by or pause to rest beneath the shade we provide.

TRAVELING MERCIES

"That through endurance and through the encouragement
of the Scriptures, we might have hope."
(Romans 15:4b)

When the American women stood in front of the Kenyan mothers in Ruiru just outside of Nairobi, they were acutely aware of one thing. Though land and language separated them, though skin color and culture varied between them, they shared a common bond. Each of them had known struggle, had been familiar with suffering, and understood that life came bundled with heartache.

The English-speaking women needed a Swahili interpreter to ensure their words were clearly understood, but they did not need any translation of the needs of each heart in that simple church structure. When the Americans shared their stories of abandonment, of illness, of life's unpredictable twists and turns, their examples resonated with the Kenyans. Light shone from their audience's eyes; humming sounds of agreement escaped through their pursed lips.

Because God asked all three Americans to walk in difficult places, to journey amidst brokenness, he carved within them a cavity that he filled with life-giving water. As they addressed the mothers seated before them, the Spirit of God was able to pour himself through the reservoir he had created inside the travelers.

In the way that a bucket draws up whatever lies within the well, the women offered refreshment drawn from the abundant hope the Lord had splurged on them.

God had sustained the travelers every step of the way; now they could quench the thirst of other souls many miles from home.

ALTERNATE ROUTE

"Look to the Lord and his strength; seek his face
always. Remember the wonders he has done."
(Psalm 105:4)

Devastating circumstances and irritating nuisances leave us befuddled, every nerve scrambling to make a point. Life jerks us abruptly, and we long to react like a toddler pitching a full -blown temper tantrum.

We can. We get to choose our response to what invades our lives. God lays out principals in his Word – he gives the Spirit to comfort and to calm – but he allows us to determine our reaction. We are given freedom to shake our fist in his face, to turn our backs and place the blame squarely in his lap. Because he knitted free will into our makeup, we may react in anger or simmer in the stew of bitterness, allowing this poison to corrode and destroy.

In Psalm 105:1-5, God offers an alternative to destructive choices. Like a physician's prescription for health, the psalmist directs us to gratitude; to calling on the name of God; to songs of praise; to recalling the wonderful works he has already accomplished.

"Look to the Lord and his strength; seek his face always" (Psalm 105:4). Keep your eyes fixed on the face of Christ. Draw your strength to manage, to cope, and to endure from his limitless resources. When the way still seems confusing, when the view ahead is blurry, go ahead and continue turning in the direction of the Lord.

That option will always prove profitable.

MAKE WAY

"I came that they may have life and have it abundantly."
(John 10:10)

Life and death walk hand in hand like comrades sharing a narrow path, jammed near each other, inhaling and exhaling the very same air. Recently, I caught them peering at one other, thriving in the cramped confines of the same cubicle. A daughter of mine, grafted into my heart three years ago, labored to draw breath, battled to bear down, every ounce of her given to the grand cause of bringing her first child into existence.

Before my eyes our miracle emerged: pale skin, perfect lips, quivering cry. Then, distinctly, I heard the strains of a new song, for my granddaughter cried, and my heart plays still that first, magical lullaby.

Seven days passed, and I watched as death wrapped its arms around life, and life triumphed over death. As my aunt struggled for breath, she labored to leave the world behind, wrestled to reach the other side. Death bore down but could not steal her away; the only part it held was her empty shell.

Beating within her heart was life made eternal by the Savior of her soul. We had watched our aunt live well, serving him wholeheartedly and sharing him continuously. Now, we witnessed as she emerged into life everlasting.

I watched two women make their way into their new world. The tiny one has just begun her days on earth. The wise one has just begun her forever in heaven. My prayer is that the first will imitate the footsteps of the second and choose to spend her years devoted to the one who is "The way, the truth and the life."

DRAGGED FORWARD

"So on the next day Agrippa and Bernice came with great
pomp...at the command of Festus, Paul was brought in."
(Acts 25:23)

Self-importance saturates those with power. The high and mighty
actually believe their own press release and often belittle those
beneath them. Throughout history, however, it is always God
who determines the ultimate outcome, regardless of the intentions
of those in authority.

In the twenty-fifth chapter of Acts we read of Paul's tedious imprisonment while he awaited the governor's decision about his release. Prominent officials instigated wicked schemes to murder the
apostle. Those with clout repeatedly forced Paul to make a defense
before them, oblivious that God was ensuring these influential men
and women heard the Gospel from the lips of their prisoner. Each
time Paul was dragged forward and forced to speak, God used the
occasion to give him a distinct platform to declare his Truth. Though
it seemed Paul was at the mercy of those in power, Christ was completely in charge.

The Creator of time and space holds today in check as well.
Despite the news filtering through the airwaves, our Sovereign God

still rules on high. He guarantees that our bewildering circumstances and unscheduled interruptions will become a platform for others to hear his voice. When our backs are against a wall and our hands tied, we must remember that his empowering Spirit is free to transform and unleash us to accomplish objectives for the Kingdom of Heaven amidst the confusion and conundrums of planet earth.

ON THE GROUND

"For whatever was written in former days was written for our instruction, that through endurance and through the encouragement of the Scriptures we might have hope."
(Romans 15:4)

S it on any airplane, and you will eventually hear these familiar remarks: "Fasten your seatbelt, locate the emergency exit nearest you, and place the oxygen mask on in the event of a change in cabin pressure." These directions are often repeated and always enforced. Sit in many pews across our land, and you may eventually hear these familiar remarks: "Make time to be alone with God, remember to pray continually, and don't neglect to read the Scriptures." Another list of directions repeated often; these are regularly ignored.

Life on the ground has its own set of pressures, and the oxygen mask of Scripture is vital for survival. Before the tilt in altitude sends us reeling, God reminds us that he left his Word as a continual channel for life.

When we carve time to be alone with God, we inhale the essential elements found in Old and New Testaments. To breathe in Scripture is to give our souls spiritual renewal and stability. Psalm 119:7 directs: "I will praise you with an upright heart, when I learn your righteous rules."

Scattered throughout this chapter's 176 verses is the encouragement to "meditate on your promises, love your commandments above gold, and stand in awe of your words." The psalmist gives us the result: "If your law had not been my delight, I would have perished in my affliction. I will never forget your precepts, for by them you have given me life" (Psalm 192:92-93).

Living Words…words to live by…words of life for living the endless life.

DEPART

"The law of your mouth is better to me than
thousands of gold and silver pieces."
(Psalm 119:72)

Not even dogs carry his name. We remember Judas Iscariot's grievous crime whenever we break the bread and sip from petite communion cups. When we press the burgundy liquid to our lips as a reminder of Jesus' spilt blood, pastors worldwide remind us of this heinous act as they quote from I Corinthians 11:23, "The Lord Jesus, on the night he was *betrayed*...."

The phrase does not read, "On the night he was denied," or even, "On the night he was scourged and crucified." As horrendous as these experiences were, none of them bears the seditious mark of Judas' betrayal: the Son of God sold for a measly handful of coins, the purchase price for a runaway slave.

Christ awoke every morning with full knowledge of Judas' future actions but never revealed it to the other eleven. Even at the Last Supper, none of the disciples suspected Judas of underhanded behavior. Judas spent three years with the Master and yet falls into the category Jesus spoke of in Matthew 7:21: "Then will I declare to them, I never knew you; depart from me, you workers of lawlessness."

The betrayer was only posing as a follower. In fact, he was the ultimate imposter, camouflaged with the outward veneer of a disciple. Paul describes those with a Judas heart as, "...lovers of self, lovers of money, proud, arrogant...having the appearance of godliness but denying its power" (2 Timothy 3:2,5).

The one who lived inches from the Messiah for over a thousand days sold him out for a pittance. Tragically, he fulfilled Jesus' haunting words: "For what does it profit a man to gain the whole world and forfeit his soul?" (Mark 8:3) May we bow our hearts before the Lord and ask him to replace anything resembling "the appearance of godliness" with a passion wholly devoted to him.

GREAT RETURN

*"So shall my word be that goes out from my
mouth; it shall not return to me empty, but it
shall accomplish that which I purpose...."*
(Isaiah 55:11)

W

e do not have the final say in what is considered a smashing success. We are mere mortals, precariously juggling scenarios and situations that leave the distinct impression things are in disarray. Our feeble attempts resemble failure as balls topple and scatter, no matter how desperately we try to keep them in midair.

The One who orders the universe and has the galaxies spinning in proper alignment has spoken. He promises that his Truth will have a radical impact, despite our perception to the contrary. In the way that it is impossible for rain and snow to descend from above without watering the earth below, it is as improbable for the Word not to accomplish his divine purpose.

This is uplifting news for the discouraged mother who faithfully pours out a helping of Proverbs along with bowls of oatmeal to her disinterested troupe, grand encouragement for the weary husband trying to influence his unbelieving wife, necessary reinforcement for the exhausted missionary seeing scanty return on his life-long investment, and motivation for the Bible teacher who is sacrificing countless time and energy mentoring young disciples with the Word.

Precipitation drenches fields and farmland and produces "seed to the sower and bread to the eater," Isaiah tells us. This is fruitfulness from heaven's outpouring to saturate earth and satisfy mankind. Likewise, God spreads his Word through imperfect people, an act that will culminate in a harvest in the lives of men and women who might not have a clue just yet that the Word will result in God's perfect purpose in their lives.

STAGGERING TOLL

"But David's heart struck him after he had
numbered the people. And David said to the Lord,
'I have sinned greatly in what I have done.'
(2 Samuel 24:10)

God branded David with the title we all strive for: "A man after my own heart." Yet even the High King David tripped over himself at times. Pride tangled his thinking like a parasitic vine, wrapping its arrogant tendrils around his clear thoughts, choking out the wisdom of humility. Pride is poison for all of us.

At the end of David's life, God reminded him of the men of valor who had accomplished gigantic feats with little resources. God brought to David's assistance "mighty men" who continually defied the Philistines, conquered eight hundred at one time, and triumphed over vast numbers of the Israelite's enemies singlehandedly (2 Samuel 23).

David, however, forgetting that the Lord was the one working out the victories, demanded a census in order to revel in the enormity of his army. It was all about David now — what he could accomplish, how many soldiers were on his side, and the smug security of relying on his natural resources. His own words condemned him: "You save a humble people, but your eyes are on the haughty to bring them down" (2 Samuel 22:28).

Down they went: 70,000 of the very men who had just been cataloged as able-bodied warriors. Although David knew immediate remorse after the count came in, the devastating consequence was still unleashed through an angel of destruction. We see David's brokenness as he cried, "Behold, I have sinned, and I have done wickedly" (2 Samuel 24:17); nevertheless, his pride took a catastrophic toll on the lives around him.

This man whose heart belonged to God teaches us great truths in the psalms he penned, in the giants he felled, and in the remorse he expressed over his failures. Perhaps one of David's finest lessons, though, is this haunting reminder of the staggering toll pride elicits. This character flaw is always a giant in need of slaying.

PART V

LIGHT FOR THE WAY AHEAD

*"Because of the tender mercy of our God, whereby
the sunrise shall visit us from on high to give light
to those who sit in darkness and in the shadow of
death, to guide our feet into the way of peace."*
Luke 1:78-79

WINGS

"As for me, I shall behold your face in righteousness…."
(Psalm 17:15)

The New Year comes full of promise, packed with potential, buzzing with beginnings and resolutions and goals. But, wait. Everything isn't new. Some things are tried and true, stable, resolute, unchanging. Truth…hope…wonder. Their brilliance penetrates the past and ushers us forward like a bright beam of light.

Truth is promise permeating all the Psalms and summarized in a succinct line of the seventeenth one: "I call upon you, for you will answer me, O God" (Psalm 17:6a). The One I appealed to for help previously, I can still depend on presently.

The Creator of yesterday, today, and forever gives us his word that he will hear us and respond. We go forward, confident that he is aware of our concerns and will act toward us like a benevolent Father. In a few simple words, we receive an enormous assurance of hope and a reminder to persevere in prayer as children expecting to hear a gracious response from a loving parent.

Allow this truth to soak inside you, and be surprised with the wonder of belonging to such a God. Then, like David, pray: " Wondrously show your steadfast love, O Savior of those who seek refuge from their adversaries at your right hand. Keep me as the apple of your eye; hide me in the shadow of your wings…." (Psalm 17:8).

Hidden beneath wings of protection, cocooned within the center of his focus — that's a great beginning for the flight forward.

VANTAGE POINT

"In the beginning, God created the heavens and the earth."
(Genesis 1:1)

Winter rears her beautiful form, shakes her magnificent mane, and startles us with her roar of wonder at beginning afresh. A new year full of sparkling hope and enduring promises is ahead, and we find delight in all things new and in old things true, tested, and sure.

Familiar lines rekindle awe; I've heard it before, but it surprises me still. In the beginning, where void was all and form was absent, God himself spoke words, and light became visible and good. Speaking more, dividing daylight and darkness, creating Heavens and Earth, he brought plant life and sea urchins and everything in between into existence.

An altogether different story line emerged as the Triune God formed mankind, repeating the phrase three times to make certain we got his point: "So God created man in his own image, in the image of God he created him; male and female he created them" (Genesis 2:27).

Bearing the mark of God himself, made in his likeness, created in his image, we are his cherished creation. What compares to such a magnificent beginning? How can we forget that his own hands formed us, lifted us out of dust, bent down to breathe his life into our lungs? Intimately and intricately wrapped, we are displayed as his finest work of art.

We belong to him, created by him and for him. From this vantage point we look ahead to whatever awaits, mindful that our powerful Creator still stands beside us as we step toward all he has lovingly planned for us this year.

SERVICE STATION

"For even the Son of Man came not to be served but
to serve, and to give his life a ransom for many."
(Mark 10:45)

Easter parades like a ripe sunrise bursting above the horizon, spilling enormous meaning over the calendar. We anticipate meandering through the familiar story and locking arms with old friends from within the pages of sacred Scripture, characters who played a pivotal role in Christ's final days on earth.

In John Chapter 12, we follow Mary as she approaches Jesus, who is reclining at a dinner in his honor. Martha is serving without complaint this time, and Lazarus, recently raised from the dead, is one of the festive party.

Mary extravagantly anoints the Master's feet with an exotic ointment imported from India, costing a year's wages. As the house fills with the perfume's aroma, Mary bends toward the Savior and with her hair wipes his feet, the very same feet that will soon stagger to the cross and be pierced with excruciating Roman nails.

Later, we learn of two other women named Mary who act as bravely as David facing Goliath. With no regard for their own safely, no thought for what might occur at the hands of the menacing soldiers, the women are "standing by the cross of Jesus" (John 19:25). His mother, his aunt, and his friend — three Marys intent on one consuming purpose ...to keep vigil with Christ as he suffers on the cross.

There is one other who acted courageously toward our Savior We know his name and his hometown and hail him as hero for shouldering the unbearable load for Jesus' sake. Simon of Cyrene is compelled to obey the harsh command of Roman rule, and yet from our vantage point he stands like a mighty warrior, a valiant comrade who helps our fatigued Savior bear the weight of the cumbersome crossbeam.

At a time in his earthly life when betrayal, mockery, and rejection are his bitter companions, when brutal force and floggings are his lot, it is worth saluting those few who offer the Lamb of God small tokens of kindness. Mary at his feet, the women waiting close by, and Simon at his side – all beckon to us from their noble position. Perhaps their examples will prompt us to replicate compassionate service in the name of our King who poured out his royal blood on our behalf.

HOPE SPRINGS

"And they were both righteous before God, walking
blamelessly in all the commandments and statutes of
the Lord. But they had no child, because Elizabeth
was barren and both were advanced in years."
(Luke 1:6-7)

On the calendar, Easter looms like a lush field of lilies. This is a worthwhile time to regain perspective, and to visualize the footsteps of the Savior on his way to the cross. Before long, just as we barely begin the story, we are made aware of gracious truth that puts life into sharper focus.

Elizabeth and Zechariah had no penalties against them. Their characters were flawless, their devotion complete. In God's eyes they were righteous, living out their faith by absolute obedience to his laws. Yet, despite such an exemplary record, they were childless in a culture that viewed this as a shameful offense. Their perfection in God's sight did not excuse them from experiencing the anguish of a vacant womb.

Obviously, their pain was not punishment or disapproval from the Father. They were struggling, but his face was not set against them.

Our disappointments do not mean that the Father is displeased with us, either. In the way he was preparing Elizabeth and Zechariah for the task of one day parenting John the Baptizer, he is orchestrating the details of our lives for his grand purpose.

God knows what he is doing and is mindful of our situation. He is at work even though we might not understand his plan. When we find ourselves in a precarious place, we must believe that God is in control, regardless.

Elizabeth and Zechariah show us that beauty comes from brokenness and that hope springs from barren ground. The cross is in view, even from here.

STATE OF HEART

"For this is my blood of the covenant, which is
poured out for many for the forgiveness of sins."
(Matthew 26:28)

S in is a three-letter word rarely used in polite society and never mentioned in daily newscasts. It masks itself in subtle ways, blazes boldly out in front, or gnaws at us like termites nibbling away at undergirding beams. Fully present just below the surface and invisible to the human eye, it makes its deceitful mark by deception and false claims.

It's precisely why we had Easter in the first place.

Christ breathed our oxygen, cried our tears, and died an excruciating death over that three-letter word. Ever since it entered the Garden, it raised an ironclad curtain preventing us from experiencing perfect fellowship with our Creator. With the cross as his pointed dagger, Christ Jesus plunged his weapon into the heart of sin and destroyed its grasp on us for eternity.

Some of us see ourselves as good and upright citizens who have tried successfully to master our longings, made ourselves presentable, and never wandered into the far country. Like the elder brother in the parable of the prodigal, we wear the garments of pride and self-righteousness. Christ declares to us, "None is righteous, no, not one...all have turned aside."[171] In other words, sin cannot be camouflaged.

Others believe themselves too far gone, beyond the reach of forgiveness; their past mistakes and prodigal years have rendered them exempt from God's cleansing. Like the prodigal who returns with the stench of the pigpen as his pungent odor, these sons and daughters straggle home, never once believing the Father's love could see them as anything more than second-class citizens.

Both the good and the bad are stained by the ugly mark of sin; both are in need of saving. And Easter is that brilliant, outlandish rescue by a God so in love with his people that he would sacrifice his very best, his only Begotten Son, on their behalf. "Behold, the Lamb of God, who takes away the sin of the world!"

Truth for us to cherish, no matter the season we are in or the state of our heart at present.

DOMAIN

*"He has delivered us from the domain of darkness and
transferred us to the kingdom of his beloved Son, in
whom we have redemption, the forgiveness of sins."
(Colossians 1:13-14)*

Easter departs, but an awareness of the gift lingers on.
Realization and wonder stir from time spent at the pierced
feet, from waiting near the wounded side of the Savior wearing a thorn -encrusted crown and wholeheartedly submitting to the
Father's will.

Blessed Jesus, you love and keep loving; you give and keep giving. You took our place, wore the onslaught of our sin, and carried
the cross to rescue us from the domain of darkness. You spent every ounce of yourself to ensure our relationship with the Father was
healed.

How can we possibly thank you for paying the price and for calling our name until we finally heard? You shelter us beneath the shadow of your wing and envelop us in your perfect protection. Loving
the unlovely, forgiving the unpardonable, you breathe out unlimited grace and strength. Rescuer from despair, filler of empty hearts,
healer of insurmountable loss, you never abandon, you never forsake.

Easter trails behind, but before us stands the cross where the great exchange occurred, where you spilled your blood to cleanse our wickedness. Righteous Ruler, you provide a path for us to be made right in your eyes. Divine King, you take residence within for us to dance to the song of the Heavenly Kingdom while we tread on the pavement of planet Earth.

Peace-making, cross-bearing, blood-shedding, penalty-paying Savior. Enough said.

CAMPING OUT

"As a father shows compassion to his children, so the
LORD shows compassion to those who fear him. For he
knows our frame; he remembers that we are dust."
(Psalm 103:13)

Barbeque coals with sizzling meat, neckties and gadgets wrapped in their unique boxes, home made cards with printed crayon script...Father's Day grants us a chance to celebrate and honor our dads for who they are, for what they've done, for who God called them to be. This is a fitting time to reflect on the God of Heaven and Earth who refers to himself as our Heavenly Father and embodies all the flawless attributes of a perfect parent.

Within the covers of every child's Bible storybook, with its picturesque illustrations, are highlights of some of his fatherly characteristics. From the very beginning, we see him as the initiator in the relationship, looking for Adam and Eve when they hide from him in the Garden, and supplying them discipline for their sin and a covering of animal skins for protection. Later, God closes the door of the ark securely with his own hand after ushering in Noah and his family. Their safety is paramount, and he supernaturally preserves their lives through the raging floodwaters.

Covering the children of Israel with an expanse of clouds during the scorching daylight hours, he also wards of wild animals and freezing nighttime temperature with a pillar of fire in the dark (Exodus 13:21) For their thirst, he orchestrates rivers of water from hard rock; for their hunger, acres of manna and quail. With the tender concern of a devoted parent, the Creator of the universe stretches out his hands to satisfy their needs.

Counseling Moses on the mountaintop, the Lord hands him clear, written instructions on precisely what is expected. As Holy God, he desires his people to live holy lives; as diligent Father, he provides them a blueprint of exact laws to ensure they are successful. With benevolence and unlimited forgiveness, he loves them even when they are complaining, discontented, cantankerous, whining children on the endless camping trip encircling the Promised Land.

King David understands God's tender compassion for his people and highlights just a sampling of his divine goodness in Psalm 145: "The LORD upholds all who are falling and raises up all who are bowed down. The eyes of all look to you, and you give them their food in season. You open your hand; you satisfy the desire of every living thing. The LORD is righteous in all his ways and kind in all his works."

Righteous and kind, lifting up and bending down, offering endless compassion, he is a Father entirely worthy of celebration, regardless of the date on the calendar or the season of the year.

TOP OF THE TOWER

*"Not that we are sufficient in ourselves to claim anything
as coming from us, but our sufficiency is from God."
(2 Corinthians 3:5)*

The best presents often come in the smallest packages. The apostle Paul showed he agreed with this succinct phrase: "Thanks be to God for his inexpressible gift!" (2 Corinthians 9:15) Gratefulness wrapped in the wonder of the matchless gift and captured in the fewest possible words.

In passage after passage of the grand book of 2 Corinthians, Paul reinforces his exuberant declaration by explaining why Christ is the Great Exchanger. From the outset we learn that he takes our sorrows and our sufferings and exchanges them for abundant comfort, so that we can transfer this comfort to others as a healing balm (2 Corinthians 1:5). He allows us to confront difficult circumstances that test our life and limb – but exchanges that hardship for reliance on his deliverance – time and time again (2 Corinthians 1:9).

The Lord is our Veil-Lifter, removing our blinders and allowing us to experience the freedom of walking by the Spirit. He takes away our spiritual blindness and hands us the remarkable gift of spiritual sight (2 Corinthians 3:16).

The stack of presents we receive through the Lord rises like a glorious tower as we learn that he trades our darkness for his brilliant light. "For God who said, 'Let light shine out of darkness,' has shone in our hearts to give the light of the knowledge of the glory of God in the face of Jesus Christ" (2 Corinthians 4:6).

Understanding that we are fragile jars of clay, the Lord exchanges our weakness for his power. We suffer affliction, but he prevents us from being crushed. We experience persecutions, but he never forsakes us. We are faced with death, but he takes those very areas and produces his Life in us.

The gifts keep on coming. He exchanges the weightiness of our trials for a glorious eternal weight that defies comparison. He gives us a heavenly building in exchange for the tattered earthly tent that housed us while we lived on earth. He became poor for us so he could give us his measureless riches. He accepted our sin as his own, handing us the transforming gift of his perfect righteousness.

The picture is clear: grace upon grace, gift upon gift. Without question, the indescribable Jesus is worthy of praise all the year through!

ON DUTY

"Blessed be the Lord God of Israel."
(Luke 1:68)

Appropriately, Thanksgiving Day precedes the season of Advent in the way a herald announces tidings of great joy. Most of the ordinary folk entrusted to participate in the Nativity, along with the myriad of angelic hosts on duty that night, declared exuberant praise to Almighty God, offering him the adoration and worship suited to a High King.

With jubilation, Mary cried out, "My soul magnifies the Lord, and my spirit rejoices in God my Savior...for he who is mighty has done great things for me, and holy is his name" (Luke 1:46,49).

Cousin Elizabeth's husband, Zechariah, regained his speech after the birth of their son, John, and his very first words overflowed with praise. Filled with the Holy Spirit, he continued his adoration: "Blessed be the Lord God of Israel, for he has visited and redeemed his people and has raised up a horn of salvation for us in the house of his servant David" (Luke 1:68-69).

After an angel of the Lord informed the shepherds of the wondrous birth of Christ, a multitude of heavenly beings joined in and praised God by saying, "Glory to God in the highest, and on earth peace among those with whom he is pleased!" (Luke 2:14) Even lowly shepherds were compelled to offer thanksgiving to God for granting them a glimpse of the Savior in swaddling clothes. What the angels said was absolutely true, and the shepherds returned from the mission "glorifying and praising God for all they had heard and seen."

Righteous, devout Simeon had the distinct pleasure of cradling Christ in his arms in the temple in Jerusalem. His words of blessing ring like an ancient bell calling us to worship alongside: "For my eyes have seen your salvation that you have prepared in the presence of all peoples, a light for revelation to the Gentiles, and for glory to your people Israel" (Luke 2:30-32).

Finally, an 84-year-old prophetess named Anna, who spent all her days and nights worshipping, fasting, and praying in the temple, caught sight of the Christ Child and could not do anything but utter thanksgiving to God.

Advent is opportunity to follow the example of the characters in Scripture who grace our greeting cards and fill our crèches. Let us lift our own voices in adoration to the indescribable Savior whose birth we celebrate all year through.

MAIN MISSION

"Christ Jesus came into the world to save
sinners, of whom I am the foremost."
(I Timothy 1:15b)

Beggars have empty hands, massive needs, and a lack of self-sufficiency. Their arms extend forward as their eyes search upward with longing for their pressing needs to be met.

At Christmas, we don't usually think about impoverished beggars. Our minds are tinsel-wrapped, and our trunks bulge with packages. We party from one buffet line to the other, plates piled high, calorie counters and budgets banished till January. Yet, with every Advent reading, with each retelling of the familiar Nativity story, we should remind ourselves precisely why he came.

We are the very ones St. Paul refers to as the "foremost of sinners." Needy, incapable of washing off the faintest stain of wrongdoing, we approach the Savior, desperate for help. As we bow before him, he extends to us mercy and grace in the form of forgiveness that transforms us into children of the Living God.

While on earth, Jesus did all things well: healing, feeding, teaching, proclaiming. However, Christ's primary mission, his reason for sacrificing and serving, was implicitly clear. In one succinct phrase

God's Word declares, "Jesus Christ came into the world to save sinners."

Such life-giving truth should ring clear like pealing church bells. Our hearts should leap at the realization that we must, at all costs, share this message. As we direct others toward him, we are actually one grateful beggar directing another hungry soul to find the choicest meat and the finest of wheat.

FRONT AND CENTER

"And they were all amazed and said to
one another, 'What is this word?'"
(Luke 4:36)

In the weeks leading up to the birthday of the King who holds dominion above all majesties, we may pay him homage by re-reading portions of his biography chronicled by St. Luke. His story is compelling and his actions worthy of contemplation. We just may discover that though the enormity of his person lies completely beyond our comprehension, he is fully present with us, longing to reveal himself as we linger in his Word.

There he is in his hometown of Nazareth, front and center in the synagogue, with scroll in hand. He reads words prophesied by Isaiah of his anointing to proclaim the greatest news the poor, the captive, and the oppressed will ever hear. Luke 4:20 reads, "The eyes of all in the synagogue were fixed on him," and we are mindful that we can imitate them here, placing Christ front and center in our Christmas celebrations, our focus aimed at him.

He moves to Capernaum and is assaulted by a man consumed with a demonic spirit. With a few pointed words, Jesus rebukes the demon and frees the captive, leaving the amazed crowd to whisper to one another, "What is this word? For with authority and power he commands the unclean spirits, and they come out!" (Luke 4:36) We are left to tremble too, to join them in wonder at the immeasurable power his Word still exudes today.

Later, when he enters the house where Simon Peter's mother-in-law lies ill, we read the phrase, " They appealed to him on her behalf" (Luke 4:38). What privilege it is that we, too, are able to appeal to him on behalf of others. We, too, can be about the business of petitioning the Most High God on behalf of the spiritually poor, blind, and oppressed around us.

In the quiet stillness of December mornings, with the tree's twinkling lights for company, we have the privilege to marvel at our Lord and receive through his Word the jeweled gifts only a King can has the right and the ability to offer. To not make the time for such treasures may prove we are pitiful and poor indeed.

SAFEGUARD

"He went to Pilate and asked for the body of Jesus.
Then Pilate ordered it to be given to him."
(Matthew 27:58)

The name of Joseph towers tall and strong, like an enormous mountain peak. Two men wore the designation with a lion's courage, fearless in the face of dire adversity, defying the desires of evil monarchs and the formidable armies of Rome.

Joseph of Nazareth was the first man to touch the Son of God with his fingertips, and Joseph of Arimathea would be the last man to touch Jesus before his resurrection. The Father called these two men to offer his Beloved Son tender compassion and fierce protection when he was in great need. In their capable hands, the Savior of the world would be safe.

In Luke chapter 2, we watched the first Joseph trekking to Bethlehem, where he would assist Mary in the delivery room of the newborn King. Together the couple would wrap Jesus in swaddling cloths and lay his vulnerable frame inside the cavity of a manger. God designated an earthly father, Joseph, to safeguard the precious life of baby Jesus.

Later in the story, we applauded the second Joseph as he appealed to Pilate for the body of our Lord. This wealthy disciple of

Christ used his powerful connections to ensure that Rome fulfilled his request. In startling contrast, he then cradled the battered, lifeless body of our Lord, wrapped him in a clean linen shroud, and laid him in the cavity of his own rock-hewn tomb.

At the very beginning, as Christ emerged into our sinful world, the loving arms of Joseph of Nazareth embraced him. At the very end, after Jesus had bled and died for sinful man, the compassionate arms of Joseph of Arimathea held him close. Two men named Joseph carried out their vital roles in exemplary style. They force us to ask: what role does the Father have for us today?

BOWED

"And Mary said, 'Behold, I am the servant of the
Lord; let it be to me according to your word.'"
(Luke 1:38)

Easter and Christmas are inseparable; words spoken in one reverberate into the other. A surrendered will is evident in both.

Mary portrays a dynamic picture of obedience, demonstrating a submissive spirit when handed a difficult assignment. The angel Gabriel announces God's directive for her to bear the Son of God. Mary's response to this colossal task is complete acceptance of the Father's will.

Much later, in the Garden, we hear a similar response from the lips of Mary's son. With his face pressed into the earthly carpet of Gethsemane and droplets of blood oozing from his forehead, Jesus begs for relief. "Father, if you are willing, remove this cup from me. Nevertheless, not my will, but yours be done" (Luke 22:42).

Had Mary relayed to Jesus Gabriel's surprising entrance into her world? Was there a time when she recounted for him this miraculous exchange and recited her obedient answer to the Father's demands?

For certain, both mother and Son had hearts that bowed before the Sovereign plan of God. They illustrate what complete surrender looks like, all the way from Christmas to Easter, and back again.

NO VACANCY

*"And she gave birth to her firstborn son and wrapped
him in swaddling clothes and laid him in a manger,
because there was no place for them in the inn."*
(Luke 2:7)

"N o room in the inn" would become a signature for how
the Son of Man would be regularly excluded from the
world he came to save. Repeatedly throughout the
Gospels, a "No Vacancy" sign was extended to Christ as he journeyed
toward the cross.

In the synagogue of his hometown of Nazareth, he stood and
read Isaiah from the scrolls and then informed the audience of their
hardened hearts. Rather than repenting, "They rose up and drove
him out of the town and brought him to the brow of the hill on which
their town was built, so that they could throw him down the cliff"
(Luke 4:29). No room for Christ in Nazareth.

When he traveled to the region of Garasenes, opposite Galilee,
Jesus healed a man the demons identify as Legion from demonic pos-
session. With his unparalleled authority, Christ sent the multitude
of evil spirits into a pig herd that rushed into the lake and drowned.
Rather than rejoicing in their neighbor's good fortune, the townspeo-
ple "Asked him to depart from them, for they were seized with great

fear" (Luke 8:37). The pigs meant more to them than the Healer's presence; there was no room for Christ in Garasenes, either.

Later, when he entered Samaria, "The people did not receive him, because his face was set toward Jerusalem" (Luke 9:53). The disciples wanted fire to destroy the city, but Jesus rebuked the twelve rather than the ones who openly rejected him.

Here again, there was no room for Jesus.

Probably the greatest rejection came from the city of Jerusalem and its religious leaders. Jesus lamented over their unbelief: "O Jerusalem, Jerusalem, the city that kills the prophets, and stones those who are sent to it! How often would I have gathered your children together as a hen gathers her brood under her wings, and you would not!" (Luke 13:34) They would not see, would not listen, would not turn and repent. From Bethlehem to Jerusalem until today – far too often, Jesus is barred from entry.

In contrast, may our lives be wide-open doorways that invites the Master to come in and make himself completely at home.

LAND LIGHT

"For my eyes have seen your salvation that you
have prepared in the presence of all peoples, a
light for revelation to the Gentiles...."
(Luke 2:30-32)

In December, the familiar may become irrelevant. What should be magical and thrilling, when viewed with an indifferent yawn becomes regular and routine. We no longer see the compelling evidence plastered like transparent tape across every Christmas card and echoing through the haunting carols.

Simeon saw the Christ Child in the temple and blessed his God for allowing him to see the Savior "of all peoples, a light for revelation to the Gentiles." Earlier, the angel had proclaimed to the shepherds "Good news of a great joy that will be for all the people" (Luke 2:10). Then a multitude of the heavenly host declared, "On earth peace among those with whom he is pleased."

Scattered throughout the well-known Christmas story is the clear proclamation that God sent his Son as Savior for the entire world. Clearly, all people from every land, and in every language, matter supremely to God: the Hindu taxi cab driver in Katmandu; the Muslim tour guide at the Taj Mahal in Agra; the lepers in their designated colony in Bangladesh; the meagerly clad toddler in the Kibera slum in Nairobi; the intellectual atheist studying at Oxford. The Christmas narrative includes them all.

The one called Light of the World delivers on his promise as Prince of Peace. Inside the darkest hovels, he beams brightly. Where misery should reign, he triumphs with hope. In lands lacerated by multiple grotesque gods, he stands supreme, bringing salvation to "all peoples" and "great joy" to faces across the globe.

Try reading the story again. This time, see the world from the Savior's point of view. That might forever change the way you look at Christmas.

ENDLESS KINGDOM

*"He will be great and will be called the Son of the Most
High. And the Lord God will give to him the throne of
his father David, and he will reign over the house of
Jacob forever, and of his kingdom there will be no end."*
(Luke 1:32-33)

I f Christmas is anything, it is God keeping his promises.
Through the lips of Nathan the prophet, God told King David,
"And your house and your kingdom shall be made sure forever
before me. Your throne shall be established forever." In Psalms 132:
11 we read the promise once more: "One of the sons of your body I
will set on your throne."

Earlier in history God had made a promise about Abraham, "I
will establish my covenant with him as an everlasting covenant for his
offspring after him" (Genesis 17:19).

When Mary opened her lips in overwhelming adoration of God after fleeing to the home of Zechariah and Elizabeth, she proclaimed,
"He has helped his servant Israel, in remembrance of his mercy, as he
spoke to our fathers, to Abraham and to his offspring forever" (Luke
1:54-55). The prophecies she had heard her whole life were being
fulfilled at that very moment within her body. As the angel Gabriel

predicted, she would bear the "Son of the Most High," who would "reign over the house of Jacob forever."

No wonder we cringe inwardly when the grandeur of Christmas is reduced to twinkling lights and merriment. Something within us longs to cry out, like Mary, "My soul magnifies the Lord, and my spirit rejoices in God my Savior" (Luke 1:46-47).

We are made to worship like Zechariah and declare, "Blessed be the Lord God of Israel, for he has visited and redeemed his people and has raised up a horn of salvation for us in the house of his servant David, as he spoke by the mouth of his holy prophets of old, that we should be saved from our enemies" (Luke 1:68-71).

Christmas is a bold and wondrous celebration of salvation from the enemy of sin and death. Christmas is a vibrant reminder that we serve a God who keeps his promises, even though it came with the highest price tag possible.

LIFE JOURNEY

"And they were both righteous before God, walking
blamelessly in all the commandments and statutes
of the Lord. But they had no child...."
(Luke 1:6-7a)

Zipping through the Christmas narrative, we may easily overlook the opening players in the drama that unfolds around the Christ Child. Writing his "orderly account," Luke first introduces us to an ordinary couple executing their normal tasks when are God Almighty invited them to play a vital role in his Son's arrival on earth.

The Lord purposefully selected a pair of old people who had been marginalized their entire marriage with the label of "childless." Zechariah and Elizabeth's prayers had been unanswered all those painful years while God has orchestrated unimaginable details to ensure they would be part of the unveiling of the long-awaited Anointed One.

God met with this common priest as he engaged in his regular duties, faithfully fulfilling his responsibility. Together with his wife, this priest had walked blamelessly before the Lord, had obediently followed the commandments and statutes of the Lord, living night and day, year after year with acute disappointment.

Ordinary and old, blameless and barren, these two would parent John the Baptizer. Their son would "turn many of the children of Israel to the Lord their God...to make ready for the Lord a people prepared" (Luke 1:16-17). For this enormously important job, God took a husband and wife, broke their hearts, crushed their dreams, and when he saw fit, fulfilled their highest desire.

It might be worth our while to consider the lives of this man and woman, "advanced in years," yet perfectly suited to carry out God's divine orders. When we feel ordinary, when our daily activities seem routine and unglamorous, when our prayers have been unanswered, let us believe that God is at work regardless. Let the remarkable life journey of Zechariah and Elizabeth cause us to yield our own hearts' desires to the Savior.

FOUND

*"And this will be a sign for you: you will find a baby
wrapped in swaddling cloths and lying in a manger."
(Luke 2:12)*

Babies are helpless, totally dependent on the care of others,
completely incapable of meeting any of their own needs.
They squawk and cry to communicate, bawl when hungry,
wail when sleep-deprived.

The incomparable High King allowed himself to be entirely vulnerable, at the mercy of his creatures, handled and held by imperfect
human beings. What kind of God would lower himself to such a de-
fenseless position?

The shepherds were instructed to find the baby, and they would
find the Savior. The angel proclaimed to them the extraordinary
news that would provide the greatest joy for every people group under heaven. The Messiah had come on a specific day to a specific
place, slicing through time and space, to be contained in flesh for
one eternal reason: to fulfill the Law perfectly and pay the ransom
price for us.

After thirty-three years of accomplishing the Father's perfect will,
when his time had come, he allowed them to manhandle and mis-
treat him because he had come to meet our needs. "Though he was

in the form of God, he did not count equality with God a thing to be grasped, but made himself nothing, taking the form of a servant, being born in the likeness of men. And being found in human form, he humbled himself by becoming obedient to the point of death, even death on a cross" (Philippians 2:6-8).

He became helpless to help us; vulnerable to vanquish sin; broken to bear the sins of the world. No wonder that one day, "At the name of Jesus every knee should bow... and every tongue confess that Jesus Christ is Lord" (Philippians 2:10-11).

The shepherds heard that good news first and "made known the saying that had been told them concerning this child" (Luke 2:17). It's still a great idea to follow their lead.

AMIDST THE RUSH

"She will bear a son, and you shall call his name
Jesus, for he will save his people from their sins."
(Matthew 1:21)

He rocked our world, granted us life of the everlasting kind, and paid the highest ransom price to free us from sin's ugly grasp. In return, what gift could possibly be worthy or suitable for the one who knows no lack or need, who exists without a wish list or a want?

Each time I cease my frantic pace, sit before his throne of grace, and pour my heart in love to him, a gift I bring, a beloved offering. When I pause amidst the rush, move aside the urgent stuff, and take the time to sit and read, to look intently at verse or phrase, to study the Word he left for us, I bring a gift to honor him.

If I would wait before I speak, still my tongue and make it cease from critical words that wound and bite, and choose instead to bless and praise, a beloved prize I bring to him, the One with no need of anything. When I think of others' needs, put aside my pressing load, seek other weary souls, and bear their burden willingly, that gift he would find sweet and right, a present becoming the God of Light.

To share his name out loud someplace, to remind anther, "God is here!" Immanuel has come; it's true; his love is rich, and his grace is good. Consider well why Jesus came, why as a babe he lay in manger frame. Ponder now the road he took, the cross he bore, the grave he shook, the death he died, the life he gives. Listen friend and allow me time to share this truth; it will change your life.

We bless your name this morning Lord, amidst the Season's roar; we hand to you these simple gifts; we long to love you more.